MW01707662

by Kelly Oliver

alpha books
A Division of Prentice Hall Computer Publishing
201 W. 103rd Street, Indianapolis, Indiana 46290 USA

 For information, address Alpha Books, 201 W. 103rd Street, Indianapolis, Indiana 46290 USA

International Standard Book Number:1-56761-371-3
Library of Congress Catalog Card Number: 93-72568

95 94 93 8 7 6 5 4 3 2 1

Interpretation of the printing code: the rightmost number of the first series of numbers is the year of the book's printing; the rightmost number of the second series of numbers is the number of the book's printing. For example, a printing code of 93-1 shows that the first printing of the book occurred in 1993.

Screen reproductions in this book were created by means of the program Collage Plus from Inner Media, Inc., Hollis, NH.

Printed in the United States of America

Publisher, Marie Butler-Knight; **Associate Publisher**, Lisa A. Bucki; **Managing Editor**, Elizabeth Keaffaber; **Manuscript Editor**, San Dee Phillips; **Cover Designer**, Scott Fullmer; **Designer**, Kevin Spear; **Indexer**, Jeanne Clark; **Production Team**; Diana Bigham, Katy Bodenmiller, Brad Chinn, Tim Cox, Meshell Dinn, Terri Edwards Mark Enochs, Howard Jones, Beth Rago, Carrie Roth, Marc Shecter

Contents

Introduction

Why WordPerfect for Windows Is Better Than Your Typewriter

It Slices, It Dices, It Even Cuts Metal

Like those knives in the commercials on television, WordPerfect for Windows can do just about anything you want it to. No more pressing return or (gasp) cranking that return bar on your typewriter. WordPerfect for Windows automatically wraps your sentences around to the next line. **Bold** letters? No problem. All it takes is a touch of a button. Need to set new tabs? A piece of cake. You could set them in your sleep.

And the best part about WordPerfect—you're going to love this—you can go back into your document and *edit,* before printing a single page. You can insert new words or new paragraphs if you want. You can delete whole sections of gibberish. If you had to do any editing on a typewritten page, you'd have to retype the whole blasted thing.

The Author Tells a Secret

I'm going to be very frank with you now: I was skeptical about WordPerfect for Windows. I mean, it seems like *everyone* knows how to use the DOS version of WordPerfect. And all those loyal WordPerfect-loving people think it's great. So it goes back to the age-old question: Why mess with a good thing?

Well, here's your answer: You mess with a good thing when you figure out a way to make it better. And that's exactly what the folks at the good ol' WordPerfect Corporation did. This Windows version is incredibly good. The newest version, 6.0, has several new features (which I'll cover in this book) that make it even easier and more fun to use.

To summarize: a WordPerfect version for Windows is the best idea since the invention of velcro. They've made the ultra-mega-powerful Windows technology available to the humongous WordPerfect audience. That's one heck of a brilliant (read: obvious) idea.

How to Use This Book

The *Complete Idiot's Pocket Guide to WordPerfect for Windows* is designed to be a friendly, easy to use manual for those of us who are short on time but who need to know the basics about using WordPerfect for Windows. Each lesson is short and to the point, but is written with a conversational tone so you won't feel like you have to read each sentence twelve times to understand it.

There are special little features like tips and figures that will help you along the way. You can look at the figures to see examples of the way your screen should look when you perform certain commands or follow a set of instructions.

The tips look like this:

Tip

> If you read one of these babies, you'll find some information that might turn out to be pretty helpful.

The following conventions are used to help you as you work through the lessons:

On-screen text	Text that appears on-screen appears in **bold**.
Menu, dialog box,	The first letter of each menu, dialog box, or window name is capitalized.
What you type	The information you type is printed in bold computer type.
What you press	The keys you press (for key combinations or commands) appear in bold.
Selection letters	The selection letter of each command or option is bold.

You can read the lessons in this book from start to finish, or you can skip around from lesson to lesson. Use this book however you feel most comfortable.

Acknowledgments

Huge thank-yous to Lisa Bucki and San Dee Phillips, who helped me whip this book into shape.

Dedication

For Jim Clinger, the nicest guy in the whole world. I wish I had written a thousand books so I could dedicate them all to Jim.

Lesson 1

Let's Start 'Er Up!

How Do I Start This Thing?

I know, I know, you're getting all antsy to dig in and start typing your document right away, but before you can use WordPerfect for Windows, you have to learn how to start it.

Lucky for you, I'm going to tell you how. First, make sure you are running Windows. Can't tell if you're running Windows or not? Here's a clue: Does it say **Program Manager** at the top of your screen? If not, you're probably not in Windows, and you have a C: prompt on your screen. (A C: prompt looks like **C:>** or some similar variation.) At this C: prompt, type **win** and press **Enter**. The Windows logo will flash on your screen, then you'll see the Program Manager window.

Tip

Yow! It Says I Have a Bad Command or File Name! If you enter the **win** command and you see the **Bad command or file name** message on-screen, that means you're in the wrong directory. You must not have the Windows directory in your path statement. You should learn how to do that. Later on, you can check your DOS manual to figure out how to add a directory to your AUTOEXEC.BAT path statement. For now, just change to the Windows directory by typing **cd\windows** and pressing **Enter**. Type **win** and you're on your way.

I've Got Windows Rolling—Now What?

Look for an icon that says something like **WPWin 6.0**. In fact, that should be exactly what the icon says unless you or someone else has changed its name. The icon will probably be in a **WP Win 6.0** program group or in your **Applications** group, depending on how your system is set up.

Figure 1.1 *Here's the little sucker you're looking for.*

Tip

What's a Program Group? If you haven't used Windows very much and aren't sure what all this gobbledygook means, turn to the back of this book, and read the very important appendix that deals with Windows basics. I put it there so people would have somewhere to turn in situations like these. I think that was very nice of me.

Okay, you've found the icon. Now just double-click on it. and wait for WordPerfect for Windows to load itself. This could be awhile. Make your grocery list, read a few chapters of a novel, write a few chapters of a novel, theorize a plan for reducing the national deficit, whatever.

And then, what we've all been waiting for . . . the WordPerfect for Windows document window! Ta-dah! Pretty cool, isn't it?

Say, This Looks Different

I suppose you want to know what all the little things are on the screen and how to use them, right? Well, it just so happens that there are several parts of the WordPerfect for Windows document window that you need to know about before we can go any further. So, even if you didn't want to know what they are, you're going to have to learn anyway.

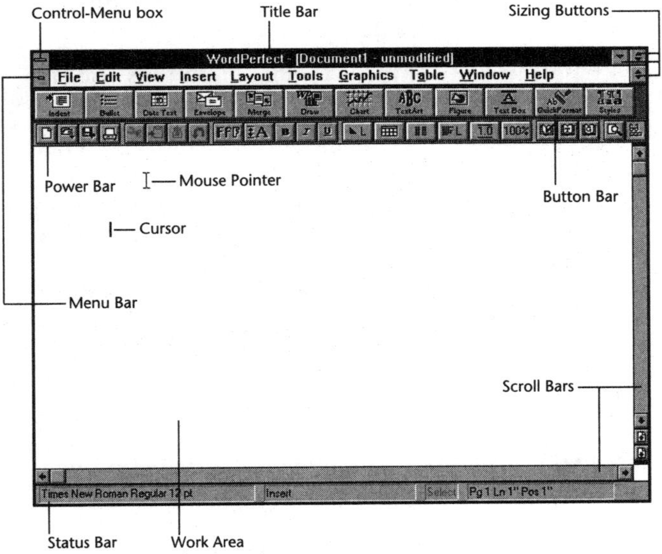

***Figure 1.2** The wonderful and glamorous WordPerfect for Windows document window.*

Control-menu box This is a standard Windows feature that's always in the top left corner of a window. When you click on it, the Control menu appears. By double-clicking on it, you can exit the current program.

Title bar This is the bar that goes across the top of the screen which tells you the name of the current document. There is a really cool trick associated with the title bar: when you move the mouse pointer to a button in the power bar, a description of what that button does appears in the title bar. Amazing!

Menu bar The menu bar is right beneath the title bar. It contains the names of the menus you can open. Menus give you choices of commands you can use. How friendly.

Button bar This is a toolbar of buttons you can click with your mouse. You can use it to quickly create a chart, insert bullets in text, indent a paragraph and so on.

Power bar A new addition to WordPerfect for Windows, this little gem contains buttons you can click with your mouse to do things like open, save and print files, and format text. Ooooh, power.

Sizing buttons See those little buttons with triangles in them in the upper right corner of the screen? You can click on them to resize your windows if they are the wrong size. What fun!

Mouse pointer If a mouse is installed on your computer, the mouse pointer appears on-screen as an I-beam when the pointer is in the work area and as an arrow when it's anywhere else.

Cursor The small, blinking, vertical line in the upper left of the screen is the cursor. Whatever you type is inserted at the cursor.

Work area The main part of the screen is the work area. This is where your text shows up when you type it.

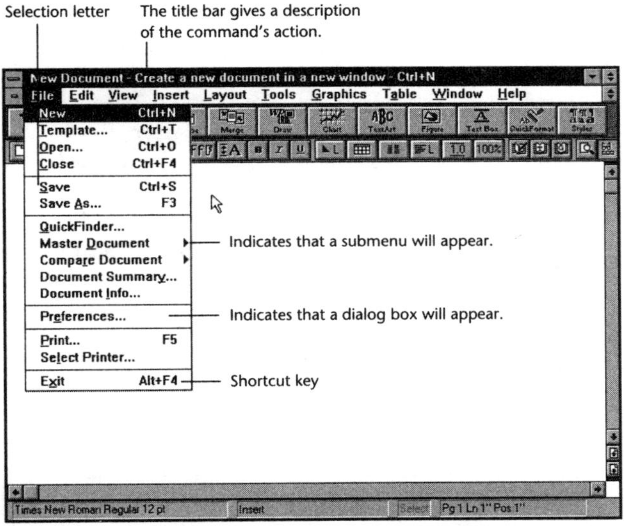

Figure 2.1 *A pull-down menu shows you a bunch of commands you can choose from.*

So How Do I Order Commands from These Fancy Menus?

To select a command from a pull-down menu using your mouse, just move the mouse pointer over the name of the menu you want to pull down, and click the left mouse button. To select a command, click on it. If the menu is pulled down and you realize you don't want to have anything to do with it, you can get rid of it by clicking anywhere outside the menu.

To select a command from a pull-down menu using your keyboard, hold down the **Alt** key, and press the underlined letter in the menu's name. (The underlined letter is sometimes called the *selection letter*, for obvious reasons.) For example, to open the File menu, press **Alt+F**. Use the arrow keys to highlight the desired option, and then press the **Enter** key, or press the selection letter in the option's name. If you decide that you don't want to use the menu after all, you can close it by pressing the **Esc** key twice. Twice? Yes, twice.

Once a menu is pulled down, you can switch to a different menu by pressing ← or →. The current menu is then closed, and the menu to the left or right is opened.

Lucky Keys and Winning Combinations

Notice how some of the commands on the File menu have corresponding keystrokes in Figure 2.1? For example, the Print command has the keystroke **F5**. Instead of opening the menu and then selecting Print, you can simply press the **F5** key. Pretty handy, eh? You can bypass the whole menu rigmarole altogether.

Menus and commands, aren't they delicious? Let's give them a big round of applause. Okay, that's enough, no time for dessert, clear the table and move along. We've got important things to cover in the next lesson.

Lesson 3

WordPerfect Dialog Boxes: In a Class All Their Own

Dialog Boxes—Poptarts of the Computer World

Dialog boxes often will pop up in your WordPerfect for Windows program. Dialog boxes aren't bad things; they're just WordPerfect's way of forcing more information out of you. In Lesson 2, I pointed out that many commands on the pull-down menus display a dialog box when selected. (You remembered that? You've got a mind like a steel trap.) For example, the File menu's **Print** command has an ellipsis after it. If you select it, you see the Print dialog box, as shown in Figure 3.1.

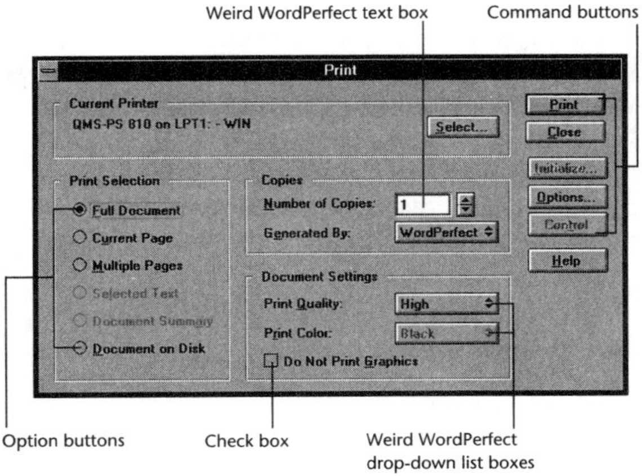

Figure 3.1 *This little morsel pops up when you select the Print command.*

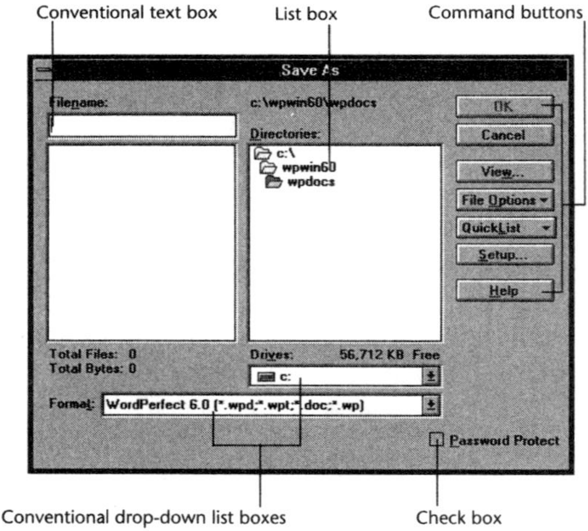

Figure 3.2 *This is the Save As dialog box. It has oodles of trendy dialog box elements in it.*

WordPerfect for Windows has its own style of dialog boxes. Some of the elements are a little bit different from usual Windows dialog boxes. Even if you think you know everything about dialog boxes, you should at least glance at these explanations, just to be on the safe side. You might find some surprises.

Look at Figures 3.1 and 3.2 for examples of all the different things dialog boxes can contain:

Option buttons These are like on and off switches. You can select only one option button in a group of option buttons. When you select one button, it deactivates the others.

Check box options More on or off devices. When you select an option, an X appears in the check box, indicating that the option is selected. To turn the option off, select it again. You can select more than one check box option in a group.

List boxes A list box contains a whole slew of stuff you can select.

Conventional drop-down list boxes Like list boxes, a drop-down list box contains lots of things. However, only one item in the list is initially displayed. To see the rest of the items, you have to pull down the list by clicking on the arrow to the right of the list. If you're using the keyboard, hold down the **Alt** key while pressing the selection letter of the list box, and then press the down arrow key.

Weird WordPerfect drop-down list boxes Sometimes, there will be two triangles on the right side of a button. That means you should point at them and hold the mouse button down to get the menu. You can drag your mouse pointer to the menu item you want, and then release the mouse button to select it. You can also use ↑ and ↓ to cycle through the list of items. So many choices.

Conventional text boxes A text box allows you to type specific information, such as the name of a file.

Spin buttons Sometimes, you'll see two little buttons to the right of a text box. They have little triangles in them. When you click on a triangle or press an arrow key, the number in the text box will go up (or down) by a specific increment. You can still type your own information into these text boxes just like normal, if you want.

Command buttons Most dialog boxes contain at least three command buttons: one for executing the command, one for canceling it, and one for getting help. If a command button has an ellipsis, that means you'll get another dialog box when you select it.

I Can't Get There from Here

To move around in a dialog box with the mouse, click on the item you want. Simple. Clicking on an option button or a check box turns the setting on or off, or *toggles* it. Clicking on the arrow to the right of a drop-down list pulls down the list. Clicking inside a text box allows you to edit its contents. Clicking on a command button closes the dialog box and executes the command. You get the idea.

Pretend that you want to use the keyboard. It's kind of a pain to use the keyboard to navigate around dialog boxes, so we'll just pretend that you want to know how. Hypothetically.

The easiest way to select a dialog box option with the keyboard is to press **Alt** and the highlighted letter in the option's name. Another way to select an option is to use the **Tab** key (or **Shift+Tab** to go backwards) to highlight the option, and then press **Enter** or use the arrow keys, if you need to.

To close a dialog box, you can press **Esc**, which is the equivalent of a Cancel key. If you cancel the dialog box, you won't be putting any of the changes you made into effect. You'll be, in essence, telling WordPerfect, "These changes I made stink. Please get me back to the edit screen and don't pay any attention to what I've been doing in this dialog box." And WordPerfect for Windows will do just that.

Okay, it looks like we've got the whole dialog box thing covered. Let's move on to a kinder and gentler topic: making your screen more friendly.

Lesson 4

The Shiny, Happy Version: Making Your Screen More Friendly

Wonder Twin Powers . . . Activate!

Form of. . . a giraffe! Shape of . . . an ice pick! Remember the Wonder Twins from the Superfriends cartoons that were on Saturday mornings a few years ago? No? Hall of Justice? Superman, Wonder Woman, Aquaman? Any of this ringing a bell? Anyway, the Wonder Twins were these two . . . well, aliens, I guess, who could change into different things by smashing their fists together and saying, "Wonder Twin Powers Activate!" Then when they were tired of being whatever they had changed into, they said, "Wonder Twin Powers Deactivate!" and they changed back into themselves.

In a way (a kind of obscure and twisted way), the WordPerfect for Windows Power Bar is a lot like the Wonder Twins. You can use it when you want to change your text into something else. You can switch around the buttons on the Power Bar and make it whatever you want. You can "deactivate" the Power Bar when you don't want it on your screen any more. Pretty heavy stuff. This is more fascinating than anything those cartoon writers could have come up with.

Where's the Power Bar and How Do I Use It?

The Power Bar is automatically on your screen when you start WordPerfect for Windows. It's right underneath the menu bar. There's a picture of it in Figure 4.1.

Figure 4.1 *Power up for WordPerfect for Windows Power Bar.*

The Power Bar is, basically, just a strip of buttons that go across your screen. When you "push" a button by clicking on it, the command that it represents is carried out. (Sorry, you can't use the keyboard for this one.) You can open files, cut text, copy text, paste text, change character formatting, and so on, with the Power Bar. If you can't tell by the picture what the button represents, move the mouse pointer so it's positioned over the button. A description of its function will appear in the title bar.

And as if all this weren't enough, you can edit the Power Bar. Oh sure, the buttons that are already on it are fine, but you can add and delete buttons, if you want. First, you select File Preferences. In the dialog box shown in Figure 4.2, double-click on the Power Bar icon (or press **Tab** until you get to it, and then press **Enter**).

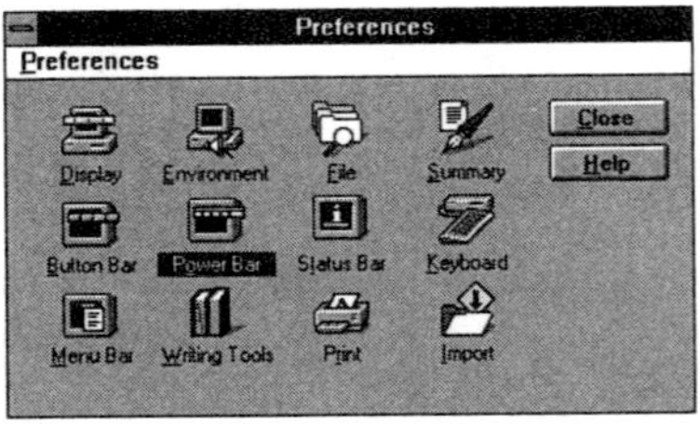

Figure 4.2 *Preferences dialog box.*

In the Power Bar Preferences dialog box shown in Figure 4.3, select the buttons you want and add or delete them. Close the dialog box when you're finished. Your new Power Bar will be displayed on-screen.

If, for some reason, you decide that you've had enough of the Power Bar, you can get rid of it by selecting View Power Bar. If you want to turn it back on later, you can use the same command.

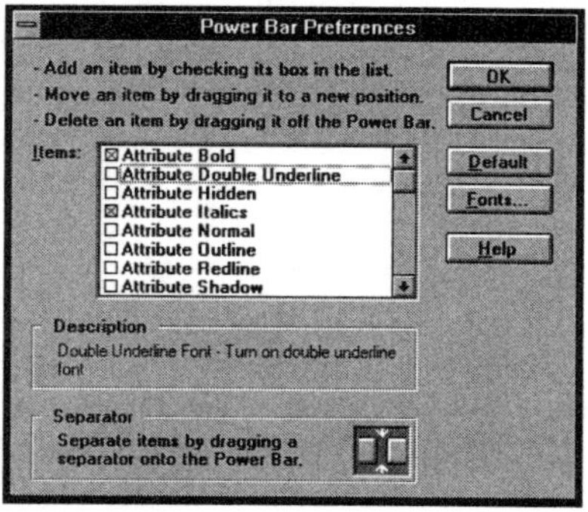

Figure 4.3 *Power Bar Preferences dialog box.*

Buttoned Down and Hanging Around a Bar

The Button Bar is similar to the Power Bar, in that you click on buttons to execute commands, and you can change the buttons in the Button Bar. A big difference between the two is that the Power Bar is mostly for common editing tasks, and the Button Bar is more specialized. For example, the default Button Bar, shown in Figure 4.4, has buttons for creating envelopes and charts, and for making indents and bulleted lists. That's a little more advanced than just opening files, I'd say.

Figure 4.4 *The WordPerfect for Windows Button Bar. Click on the button you want to use.*

The Button Bar is automatically turned on when you start WordPerfect for Windows, just like the Power Bar. You can turn it off if you want, though. It's simple; just select **V**iew **B**utton bar. Voilà.

Similar to the Power Bar, you can edit the Button Bar. However, you can't add any old button. (Actually, you can, but it's pretty complicated. We'll skip it.) Button Bars come in premade sets. You can choose a new Button Bar, like Fonts or Layout, with the Button Bar Preferences dialog box.

Select **F**ile Pr**e**ferences. In the dialog box, double-click on the **B**utton Bar icon (or press **Tab** until it's highlighted, and then press **Enter**). In the Button Bar Preferences dialog box (see Figure 4.5), click on the set you want from the list box. When it's highlighted, the new Button Bar will appear on the screen so you can see what it looks like. When you've found the one you want, click on **S**elect, and then Close.

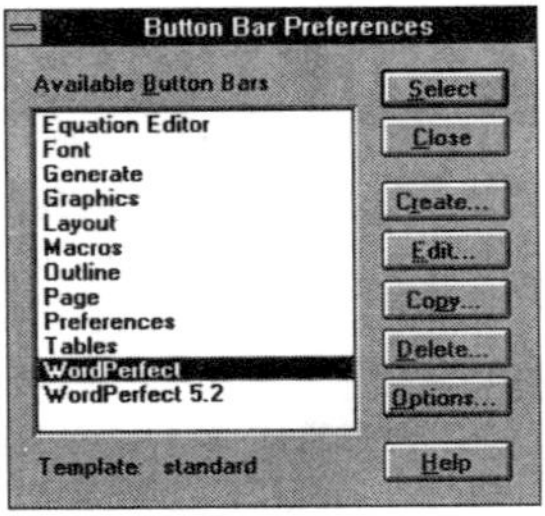

Figure 4.5 *Button Bar Preferences dialog box.*

Wow! A Built-In Ruler!

Yes, it's true, WordPerfect for Windows also has a Ruler Bar that comes in handy when setting tabs and changing margins. That's all you'll probably use it for, so it's not necessary to have it on all the time. But when you want to turn it on, use the **V**iew **R**uler Bar command.

Look at Figure 4.6. See those triangles that run along the bottom of the Ruler Bar? Those are your tab stops. If you want to change them, just drag the triangle to a new location. Pretty basic, huh?

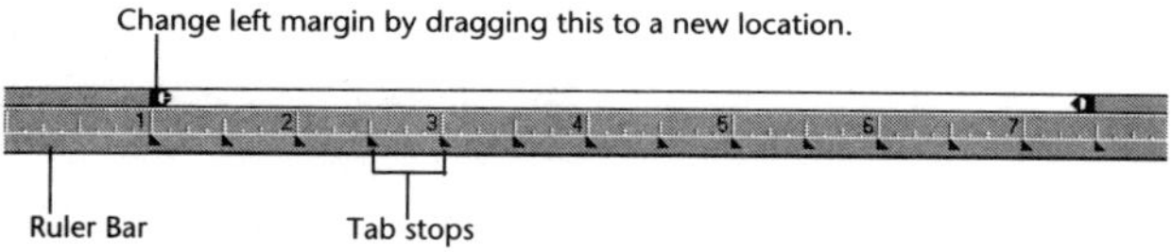

Figure 4.6 *The Ruler Bar provides an easy way to set tab stops and margins with the mouse.*

Look at the figure again. There's a doohickey above the inch marks that you use to set the margins. You can drag the ends of that bar to wherever you want the margins to be. But be warned: be careful of where your cursor is when you change your margins. The new margin settings will affect the paragraph your cursor is currently in and all following paragraphs. It won't, however, affect the paragraphs before the cursor.

Well, now that we've made the WordPerfect world seem very pretty and friendly, let's learn how to get help when WordPerfect for Windows is not so pretty (or friendly).

Lesson 5

Help!

Sending Out an S.O.S.

Sometimes, you can look at the status line for help in getting out of a jam. But for the times that you need a megadose of help, open the **Help** menu, and choose one of the options. You can select from:

Contents—Selecting this option displays a list of general help categories, as shown in Figure 5.1. Use the arrow keys to highlight a category, and press **Enter**, or click on the desired category.

Search for Help On—This option displays an alphabetical list of help topics. Use the arrow keys to highlight a topic, and press **Enter**, or click on the desired topic.

How Do I—The How Do I option takes a more practical view of help topics. It groups the help topics in logical categories, such as Basic Layout and Macros, and lists the topics in a way in which you are likely to ask for help—for example, How do I save a document? Great, huh?

Macros—The Macros option provides a list of help topics specifically for creating macros.

Coach—Coaches are on-line tutors that lead you through the process of performing a given task. Unlike real coaches, no whistle-blowing or yelling is involved.

Tutorial—The Tutorial option lets you to work through several lessons that teach you the WordPerfect basics. You probably won't need to deal with this particular feature because you already have this handy-dandy book.

About WordPerfect—This option displays some general information about the WordPerfect program. If you entered your registration number during installation, the information screen also displays this number.

Tip

Macro Schmacro A *macro* is a popular techno-computer nerd word intended to intimidate the novice. It is also a collection of recorded keystrokes or menu selections that you can play back simply by pressing a key combination or by selecting the macro from a menu. You can record dozens of keystrokes in a macro and play them back simply by pressing two keys. Macros are great for eliminating keystrokes for repetitive work. You can make a macro for names, addresses, letter closings, instructions, and oh so much more. Macros are the best thing since staple removers.

When you're really in a pickle, remember the magic help key: **F1**. To get help for a task you are currently trying to perform, start performing the task until you get to the point at which you need help. Then, press the **F1** key. This is called *context-sensitive* help. It's like a life preserver when you're sinking in a document.

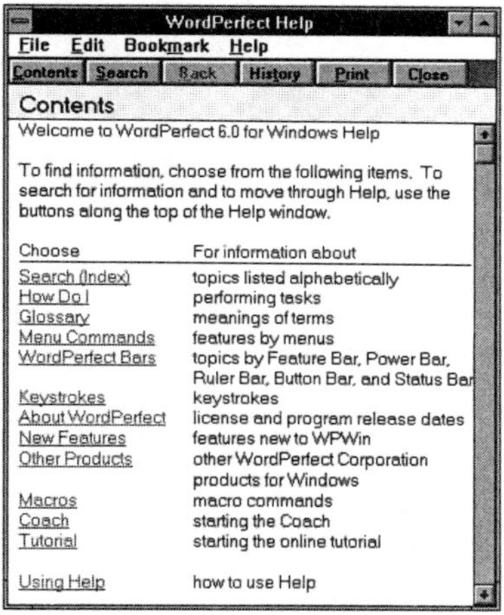

Figure 5.1 *Select the desired topic from the list of topics.*

Are you ready to learn how to quit WordPerfect when you're done with it? Keep reading.

Lesson 6

When It's Time to Quit and Go Home

Get Me Outta Here!

Had enough of WordPerfect for Windows for one day? When it's time to quit, the easiest way is to double-click on the **Control-menu box**. If you have one or more documents open that haven't been saved, a dialog box like the one in Figure 6.1 will pop up, prompting you to save the document. You can select Yes to save it, and then give it a name in the Save As dialog box that appears (more on saving in Lesson 12). You can also select No if you don't want to save it, or you can click on **Cancel** to quit the exit process.

Another way to exit is by opening the File menu and selecting Exit. Again, if you have open documents that haven't been saved, WordPerfect for Windows prompts you to save them.

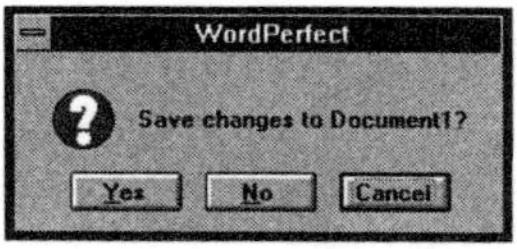

Figure 6.1 *This dialog box will appear if you are trying to exit the program without saving open applications.*

Tip

Fast Getaway To exit with the keyboard, press **Alt+F4**. This is a pretty universal shortcut key for exiting Windows applications.

Short but sweet; you've learned how to exit WordPerfect for Windows. Now let's dig in and learn how to enter text. This promises to be a good time.

Lesson 7

Entering Text Like a Whirling Dervish

How Do I Make a Document?

I'm sure the first question on your mind is this: What the heck is a whirling dervish? Well, it's a phrase used to describe the devotional practices of a particular type of Muslim monk. They dance around until they are in a trance-like state. No joke. But the more slangish meaning is something that whirls around and wreaks havoc.

> **Tip**
>
> **Trivia, Anyone?** In case you haven't memorized all the words to the songs from *The Sound of Music* (like I have), Maria was described as a "whirling dervish" by some skeptical nuns. Thought you might like to know that.

To avoid making your document look as if it were typed by a whirling dervish, there are a few things you should know about WordPerfect for Windows. Basically, you just start typing. The characters you type appear on-screen, and the cursor (the blinking vertical line) moves from left to right across the screen.

But there are some very important WordPerfect rules to know (great, more computer stuff to remember):

- Press **Enter** only to end a paragraph or a short line. WordPerfect for Windows automatically wraps text from the end of one line to the beginning of the next as you type (see Figure 7.1).

- Press the **Tab** key at the beginning of a paragraph to indent the first line of a paragraph.
- You cannot use the down arrow key to move down until you have some text to move down to. Press the **Enter** key if you want to move down.
- Any text that won't fit on the screen scrolls off the top of the screen. The text is still there (whew); you just can't see it.
- You can use the scroll bars to move to an area of your document that is not currently on the screen.

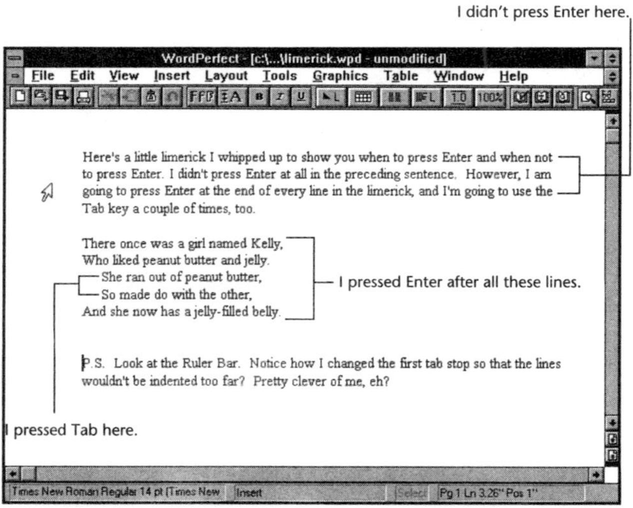

Figure 7.1 *As you type, WordPerfect wraps text from one line to the next.*

Tip

Hey! I Can't Read What I'm Typing! If your text is too small to read, open the **V**iew menu, select **Z**oom, and select the desired zoom percentage (150% works well). You can also use the **Zoom** button on the Power Bar. Instead of clicking it, hold the mouse button down and drag the mouse pointer to the zoom percentage you want. When you release the mouse button, the new zoom percentage will be selected.

Now We're Moving: Getting Around in a Document

Once you have some text on-screen, you can start moving the cursor around inside the document. To move around with the keyboard, use the keys listed in Table 7.1.

Table 7.1 Cursor-Movement Keys

Press	To Move
↑	Up one line
↓	Down one line
←	One character to the left
→	One character to the right
Ctrl+→	One word to the right
Ctrl+←	One word to the left
End	To the end of the current line
Home	To the left edge of the current line
PgUp	To the top of the screen
PgDn	To the bottom of the screen
Ctrl+Home	To the top of the document
Ctrl+End	To the bottom of the document

Using the mouse to move around in a document is more intuitive. To move the cursor with the mouse to a place you can see on the screen, just click on the place with the left mouse button.

What Are These Bars Over Here For?

Ah, the WordPerfect scrolls, a monumental archeological find. You'll like these. Some users find it easier to scroll around in a document using *scroll bars*, as shown in Figure 7.2. The horizontal scroll bar lets you scroll text from left to right across the screen. The vertical scroll bar lets you view text that has scrolled off the top or bottom of the screen.

To use the scroll bars, you can click on the arrow at the end of the scroll bar to scroll one line or character at a time. To scroll continuously in the direction of the arrow, hold down the mouse button.

You can also drag the scroll box in the scroll bar to move to the same relative location in the document. For example, if you drag the scroll box to the middle of the scroll bar, you'll be in the middle of the document. Are we having fun now?

Click inside the scroll bar, on either side of the scroll box, to scroll one screenful of text in the direction of the click. For example, if you click above the scroll box in the scroll bar, you move to the previous screenful of text. Neat, huh? Aren't you glad they dug these scrolls up?

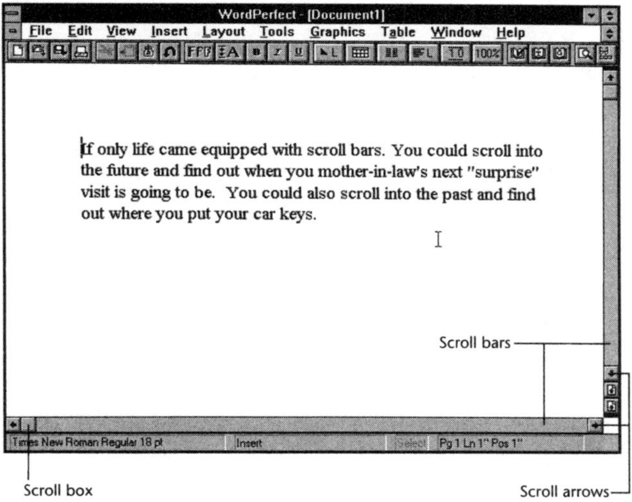

Figure 7.2 *Scroll bars can help you move around in a document.*

Inevitably, after you've created a document, you'll have an occasion to change it. Turn the page, and I'll show you how to edit.

Lesson 8

Fixing the Text You Entered Like a Whirling Dervish

For My Next Trick, Inserting Text

Editing text is a lot like performing magic tricks. You can make your text disappear (and reappear), and you can move things all around with no strings or wires. You don't even need an assistant.

You can insert text anywhere in a WordPerfect for Windows document. For example, you may want to insert a sentence in the middle of a paragraph or add a word to the beginning of a paragraph.

To insert text, move the cursor where you want the text inserted, and type the text. As you type, WordPerfect moves the existing text to the right and rewraps the text. Simple!

Tip

The Magical Typeover Mode To type over existing text, press the **Ins** key to change from Insert to Typeover mode. Everything you type will replace what is on the screen until you press the **Ins** key again. When you're using Typeover mode, the Tab key will move from one tab stop to the next, but it won't indent the text. You'll have to change back to Insert mode to do that. Watch the status bar; it will tell you what mode you're in.

The Old Disappearing Text Routine

Deleting text is a snap. Later on, you'll learn how to delete big blocks of text. However, to make minor corrections, you can delete individual characters or words by moving the cursor to the left of the character you want to delete and pressing the **Del** key.

You can also move the cursor to the right of the character you want to delete and press the **Backspace** key. To delete a word, move the cursor to any character in the word you want to delete, and press **Ctrl+Backspace**.

To delete from the cursor position to the end of a line, move the cursor to the place where you want to begin deleting, and press **Ctrl+Del**.

Whoopsy-Daisy, I Didn't Mean to Delete That

As you delete text, WordPerfect stores your last three deletions in a temporary holding area. You can undelete the text by first moving the cursor where you want the undeleted text inserted, then pressing **Ctrl+Shift+Z**. You can also open the Edit menu and select Undelete.

The Undelete dialog box appears, and the most recently deleted text is highlighted in the document, as shown in Figure 8.1. To view a previous deletion or the next deletion, select Previous or Next. The deleted text appears highlighted in the document. When you see the text you want to undelete, select Restore.

The Amazing Undo: For Those Times When You Really Bungle Everything

You may have noticed that the Edit menu also contains an Undo command. This command will undo the previously entered command, but will undo *only the last command*. If you accidentally delete text and immediately realize your mistake, you can restore the text by selecting Undo from the Edit menu or by pressing **Ctrl+Z**. WordPerfect will automatically undo the action without asking you to confirm.

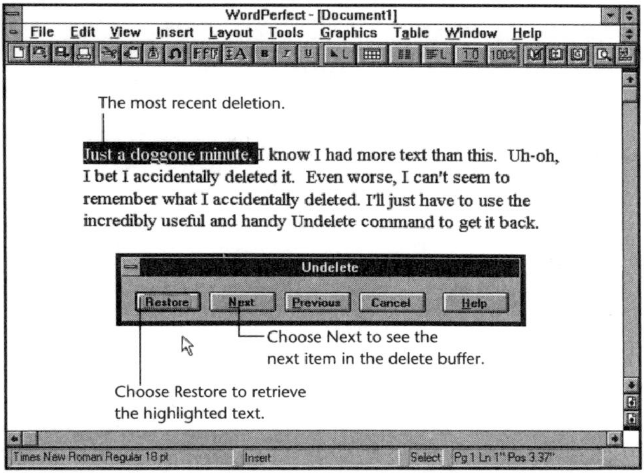

Figure 8.1 *You can restore the three most recent deletions.*

Editing in WordPerfect is as easy as pulling a rabbit out of a hat, but you ain't seen nothing yet. Now you're going to learn how to select text.

Lesson 9

Selection, Please

I'll Take the Middle Square to Block, Peter

What's a text block, you may be asking. A text block consists of any text that you select or highlight. When you select a section of text (a character, word, sentence, or other selection), you form a text block, as shown in Figure 9.1. When you have something selected, whatever command you select will be performed on the text block, such as deleting or copying the text, changing the margins for the text block, or even making the text bold or italic.

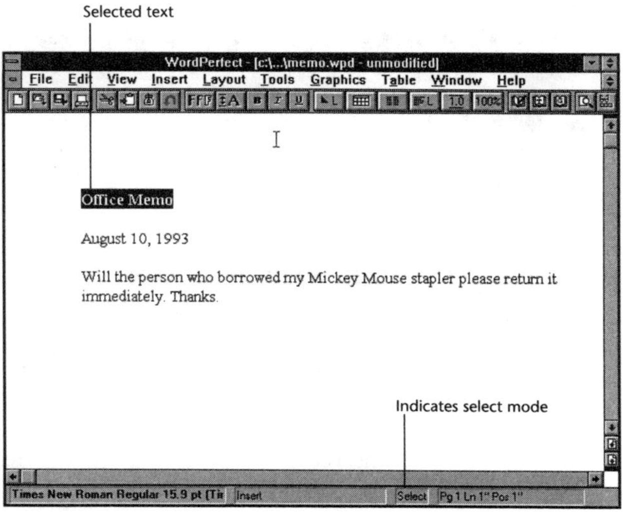

Figure 9.1 *To work with text, you must first select the block you want to work with. Makes sense.*

Selecting a Block with the Keyboard

To select a text block with your keyboard, first you have to move the cursor to the beginning or end of the block you want to mark. This position is your pivot point, allowing you to stretch the highlight over the text. Then, press **F8**. The word **Select** will become black in the status bar. (It was gray before.) This means that you are in Select mode. I guess it's kind of like the Twilight Zone.

Use the arrow keys to move the cursor to the opposite end of the block you want to select. The text is now selected, and you can perform a block operation on the text; for example, you can make the text bold, delete it, or change its alignment. Whatever you want.

Tip

Faster Than a Speeding Bullet Although you can stretch the highlight by using the arrow keys, you can also use those handy keyboard movement keys you learned in Lesson 7. For example, to select to the end of the line from the cursor position, press **F8** and then **End**. Couldn't be easier.

Selecting a Block with the Mouse

If you have a mouse, you can use the mouse to stretch the highlight over the desired text by moving the mouse pointer to the first or last character you want to select, and then holding down the mouse button. This anchors the cursor. Drag the highlight to the opposite end of the block, and release the mouse button. The selected block appears highlighted.

I Want to Select More Than a Line at a Time

Although stretching the highlight over text is the most precise way to select text, you may want to work with bigger units of text: sentences, paragraphs, and pages. If you move the cursor anywhere inside the thing you want to select, open the Edit menu and choose Select, the Select submenu will appear, as shown in Figure 9.2. Select Sentence, Paragraph, Page, or All, depending on what you want. The sentence, paragraph, or whole thing appears highlighted.

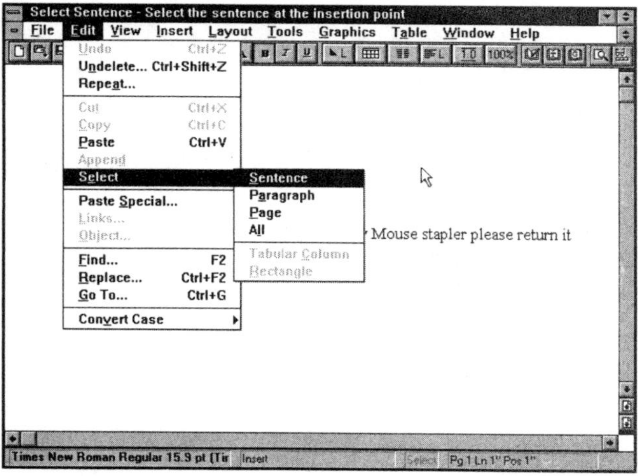

Figure 9.2 *The Select submenu allows you to work with logical units of text.*

In case you were wondering, the last two options on the Select submenu, Tabular Column and Rectangle, allow you to select text in vertical columns, rather than text that is wrapped, as in a paragraph.

Make Your Selection from the Bar

There is yet another way to select text in WordPerfect for Windows. You can use the selection bar. Don't look for it because it's invisible. You can't see it on your screen or in Figure 9.3. But it's there.

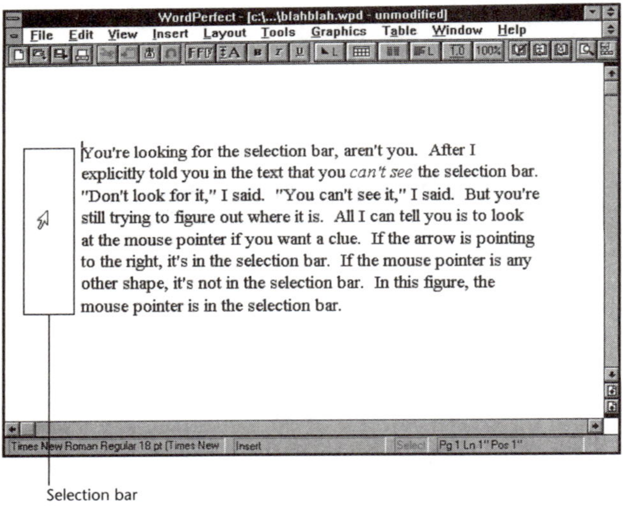

Figure 9.3 *The selection bar. (Don't worry, I can't see it either.)*

How can you tell? Well, move your mouse pointer to the left of a line or paragraph of text. See how the arrow is pointing to the right instead of to the left like it usually does? That means you're in the selection bar. If you click, the whole sentence next to the mouse pointer will be selected. If you drag the mouse pointer through the selection bar, every sentence you drag next to will be selected.

If you click the right mouse button when the pointer is in the selection bar, a QuickMenu will pop up. (Remember those from Lesson 2? I told you we'd be talking about them soon.) It has some options you can choose that pertain to selecting text. Very handy.

Now that we're done with this selecting business, I'll let you in on a little secret. All along, I've been preparing you for the next lesson, in which you'll learn how to cut and copy the text you just selected. I'm such a little trickster. Gotta love me.

Lesson 10

Cutting, Copying, Pasting, Curling, Styling

Just a Little off the Top, Floyd

Before you start *deleting, cutting,* and *copying* text, let me explain the difference between these three actions. Have a seat here.

Delete removes the text block from the document and puts it in the *delete buffer,* which holds the three most recent deletions. You can press **Ctrl+Shift+Z** to restore the block.

Cut removes the text block from the document and places it on an unseen Clipboard. You can then paste the text block from the Clipboard into another document or somewhere else in the same document.

Copy leaves the text block in the document and places an exact duplicate on the Clipboard. You can then paste the text block into another document or somewhere else in the current document.

Tip

The Invisible Clipboard Think of the Clipboard like one of those storage facilities that you can rent when you run out of room in your garage. You can store your belongings (your text) in another place temporarily until you find the place where it's supposed to go. The only weird thing about the Clipboard is that it only keeps the very last thing you cut or copied to it. That would be like a storage place that

continues

continued

throws all your old stuff down a chute in the back whenever you put something new in it. (I can't imagine that a place like that would get much business.)

Surgical Removal of Textus Blockus

To delete a section of text, first select the text block, as explained in Lesson 9. Then, press the **Del** or **Backspace** key and Presto! The selected block is deleted. A surgeon couldn't have performed a more precise removal!

Uh-Oh, I Didn't Mean to Delete That

Now you've done it. You accidentally deleted a very critical part of your document. But guess what? It's not really gone! You can get it back. You can use the Undo command from the Edit menu if the delete blunder was the *very last* thing you did.

The Undelete command, on the other hand, lets you recover your *three* most recent deletions. To undelete text, move the cursor where you want the text inserted, and press **Ctrl+Shift+Z.** You can also select Undelete from the Edit menu.

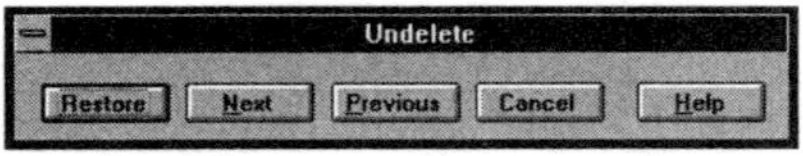

Figure 10.1 *Use Undelete to restore one of your three most recent deletions.*

The Undelete dialog box will appear, as shown in Figure 10.1. If the text you want to restore is showing, choose Restore. If not, choose Previous or Next to find it, and then choose Restore. The text will be restored wherever your cursor is, so I hope you had it in the right spot.

Cut and Clip to the Clipboard

To cut a text block and place it on the Clipboard, first mark the text block you want to cut. Then, press **Ctrl+X**, or open the **Edit** menu (see Figure 10.2) and select **Cut**. The selected text is removed from the document and placed on the Clipboard. You can now paste the block somewhere else in the document.

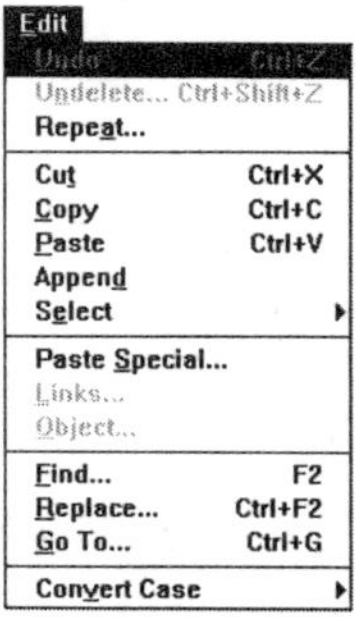

Figure 10.2 *The Edit menu contains the options for cutting, copying, and pasting blocks.*

Tip

You Just Want a Trim? Another way to cut and paste is to select the text block and then press **Shift+Del**. The block is removed from the document. Move the cursor where you want the block pasted, and press **Shift+Ins**.

Copy Some Text to the Clipboard

To copy a text block from your document to the Clipboard, first select the text block you want to copy. Then, press **Ctrl+C**. Or open the **E**dit menu and select **C**opy. The text remains in the document, and a copy of it is placed on the Clipboard.

Tip

A Snappy Copy and Paste Here's another copy and paste tip. A fast way to copy and paste is to select the block and then press **Ctrl+Ins**. Move the cursor where you want the block pasted, and press **Shift+Ins**.

If you want to copy a block to the Clipboard without replacing the block that's already on the Clipboard, select the block, and then open the **E**dit menu and select Appen**d**. The block is tacked onto the end of the Clipboard. When you paste it, the whole thing will show up.

Paste It from the Clipboard

Once you have cut or copied a block to the Clipboard, the block remains there until you quit WordPerfect or cut or copy other text to the Clipboard.

You can paste the Clipboard's contents anywhere else in the same document, or in a different document, by moving the cursor where you want to paste the block. (To move to a different document window, select it from the **W**indow menu. You can use the **F**ile **O**pen command to open a document if you need to.) Press **Ctrl+V**, or open the **E**dit menu and select **P**aste. The block is pasted at the cursor location.

Are you pleased with the result of all your cutting and styling? You're looking good; let's move on to our next appointment.

Lesson 11

Searching for That Special Something

I Know It's Around Here Somewhere

Eventually, you'll find yourself in a few situations when you'll need to find a particular piece of text in your document. Say you write an essay or an article, and you notice that you have overused the word "stuff." You want to use some other words (such as things, items, or junk) in place of the word stuff in various places. You can use the Find feature to find each occurrence of the desired term, and then you can type a new term in its place.

You can also use the Find and Replace feature to replace each occurrence of the word "stuff" with a different word (such as belongings or supplies). WordPerfect for Windows searches the document for each occurrence of a term and then replaces it with the specified term in a matter of seconds.

Searching for a Text String

Just like a detective, WordPerfect can find any text or formatting code in a document. To search for text, move the cursor where you want the search to start. You can search forward or backward from this position. (To start from the beginning of the document, press **Ctrl+Home**.)

Then, press **F2**, or open the Edit menu, and select Find. The Find Text dialog box appears, as shown in Figure 11.1. Type the text you want WordPerfect to search for. If you want, choose one or more of the options from the menus on the dialog box's menu bar.

If It Looks Like a Window and Acts Like a Window The Find Text dialog box is actually a window, not a dialog box. It can be moved around on your screen. It even has menus and everything. It's just like any other window. You can even edit text in your document while the Find Text dialog box is still on your screen. Completely ingenious.

You can use the Match menu to tell WordPerfect to look for a whole word or a certain font or code. The Options menu has a command you can choose to tell WordPerfect to start the search at the top of the document. Play around, and find the options you want.

When you've finished with all the gritty details, press **Enter**, or click on Find Next to start the search. WordPerfect hunts down the first occurrence of the specified word or phrase and selects it. To search for the next occurrence of the word or phrase, press **Enter**, or click on Find Next again.

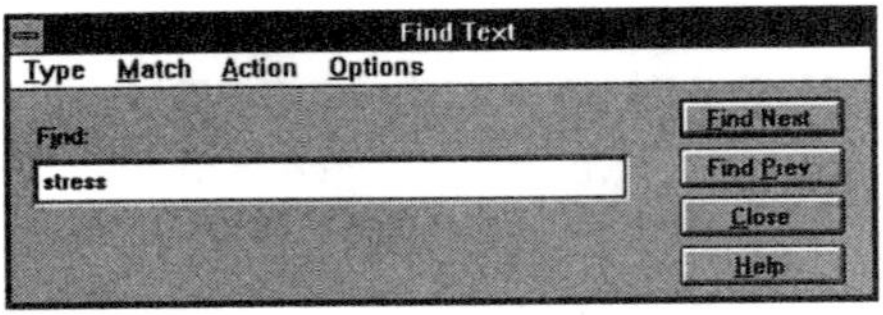

Figure 11.1 *Use the Find Text dialog box to specify the text you want to find.*

Switched at Birth: The Heartfelt Saga of the Replaced Text String

The Replace feature allows you to replace one word, phrase, or code with another word, phrase, or code. To replace stuff (I mean, items, things or junk), first move the cursor where you want the search and replace operation to start. WordPerfect searches and replaces from the cursor position forward or back.

Press **Ctrl+F2**, or open the **E**dit menu, and select **R**eplace. The Find and Replace Text dialog box appears, as shown in Figure 11.2. In the F**i**nd text box, type the text you want to replace. Press **Tab**. The cursor moves into the Replace **W**ith text box.

Type the text you want to insert in place of the F**i**nd text. Select any of the other replacement options from the menus, as desired, to control the search and replace operation. Select the **R**eplace button. WordPerfect performs the replace operation as specified.

If you just choose **R**eplace, WordPerfect for Windows will highlight the word when it finds it. If you want to replace it, click on **R**eplace. If not, select **F**ind to find the next occurrence. If you select Replace **A**ll, WordPerfect doesn't wait for you to confirm, it just replaces every occurrence of the word.

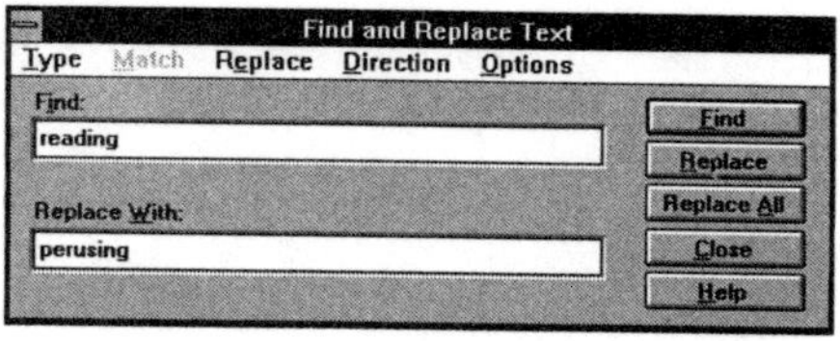

Figure 11.2 *Use the Find and Replace Text dialog box to specify your preferences.*

Now that you've got WordPerfect trained to find and replace things, I'll teach you how you can train it to save a document. And after that, I'll show you how to make WordPerfect fetch the morning paper. Move over Rover!

Lesson 12

Save a Document, Save a Life (Mainly Yours)

Why Do I Have to Save My Documents?

Saving documents is one of the best features of word processors. You can save your creation and open it up a week later, exactly as you left it, and make new changes. If you don't save your work, it will be deleted from your computer's temporary memory (RAM) as soon as you exit WordPerfect for Windows.

Sa-V-ety Rules and Regulations

You *have* to name a file when you save it. And, because WordPerfect for Windows has to follow the ugly and nasty DOS guidelines for saving files, so do you. (Bummer!) When naming a file, remember these things:

- A file name consists of a base name (up to eight characters), a period, and an optional extension (up to three characters).
- You can use any characters in the base name and extension except the following:

  space + = | \ / , [ ] : ; ? *

Where Is It Saved To?

Unless you specify otherwise, WordPerfect saves your document on the *drive* and *directory* designated in the Default Directory option of the File Preferences dialog box (which you will learn about later in this lesson).

Tip

What Are Drives? A drive is the device that reads and writes data to and from a disk. Your computer has a hard drive (usually called C), and probably has at least one floppy drive (they're usually called A and B). The hard drive contains the hard disk, which you can't remove. You put floppy disks (which you obviously can remove) into the floppy drives.

Tip

Okay, Then What Are Directories? These are different things altogether. *Directories* form the organizational structure of your disks. Related files are stored in separate directories. For example, you have a WPWIN60 directory. Your WordPerfect for Windows files are kept here so your computer knows where to look for them. Your document files are grouped into a *subdirectory* of the WPWIN60 directory called WPDOCS. If you want to know more about disks, directories, and the like, get *The Complete Idiot's Pocket Guide to DOS*, which was written by the same computer geek who wrote the words you are reading at this very second.

To save the file on a different drive or in a different directory, you must type a path to that directory in the appropriate text box (or click on the directory and drive in the list boxes). For example, if you wanted to save a file in the **OINK** subdirectory of the **PIG** directory, and name it **PORKY.WPD**, you would type:

C:\PIG\OINK\PORKY.WPD

Tip

Am I on the Right Path? A path is a drive letter, a colon, and the directories that lead to the directory in which you want to save the file. The directory names are separated by a backslash (\).

How Do I Save? Let Me Count the Ways

To save a document for the first time, first open the File menu, and select **S**ave. The Save As dialog box appears, as shown in Figure 12.1. In the File**n**ame text box, type a name for the file. (You can add a path before the file name to specify the drive and directory where you want the file saved, or you can select them from the **D**irectories and Dri**v**es list boxes.) Then, press **Enter**, or click on the **OK** button with your mouse. WordPerfect saves the document to disk and displays the documents location and file name in the window's title bar. Isn't that slick?

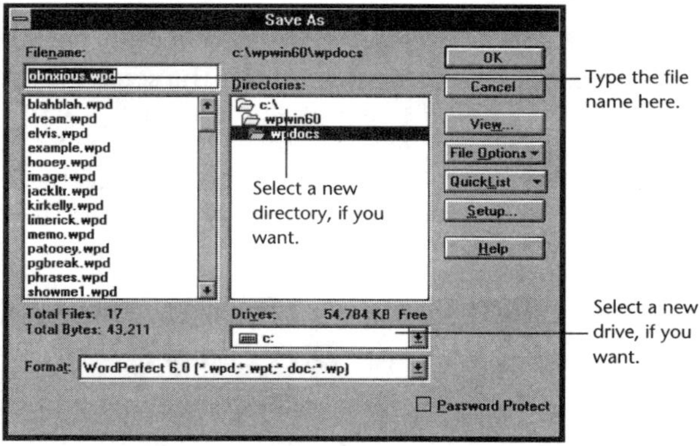

Figure 12.1 *The Save As dialog box prompts you to name the file.*

What If I've Already Saved It?

Listen up, when you save a document, only its current contents are saved to disk. If you add or delete text or change the document in some other way, those changes are stored only in your computer's temporary memory. To prevent your changes from getting lost, you should save your document regularly to disk. To save a document that you have already named, you can either select Save from the File menu, or you can simply press **Ctrl+S**. You can also click on the **Save** button on the Power Bar. Decisions, decisions.

Tip

What's the Story with This Save As Command? The Save **A**s command on the **F**ile menu lets you save a copy of the current file using a different file name. You can then edit the copy without changing the original file. Clever, huh?

I Want to Get the Whole Blasted Thing Off the Screen

To save a document and clear the screen (so you can start creating a new document), press **Ctrl+F4**, or open the File menu, and select Close. A dialog box will appear if you haven't saved the most recent changes. When you select Yes and save it, the whole blasted thing is off your screen. Adios.

Can I Tell WordPerfect to Save All My Files to One Directory?

Sure. If you save most of the document files you create in the same directory, you can set up that directory as the default. Then, you don't have to type a path every time you save or open a file. It's a pretty smart thing to do, actually.

To specify a new default directory, you must first create the directory at the DOS prompt or from within Windows. (See your DOS or Windows documentation if you need to learn how to create a directory.) After you've done that, open the File menu, and select Preferences.

The Preferences dialog box will appear. Select the File icon by double-clicking on it or by pressing **Tab** until you get to it, and then pressing **Enter**. The File Preferences dialog box will appear, as shown in Figure 12.2.

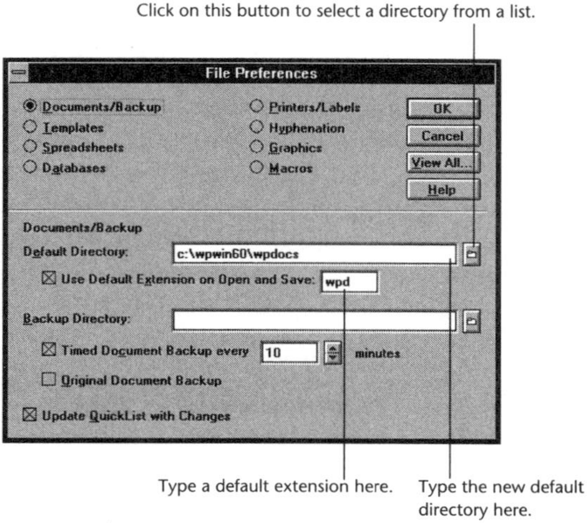

Figure 12.2 *The File Preferences dialog box in all its glory.*

Tab down to the Default Directory text box (or just click on it), and type in the path and directory name that you want to use. You can also specify a default extension in the text box right beneath it. When you're done, select **OK**.

If your WordPerfect program is ready for more obedience training, turn to the next lesson, and teach it to open and retrieve documents you've already saved and want to work on again.

Lesson 13

Teaching WordPerfect for Windows to Fetch

Opening or Inserting a Document—What's the Difference?

When you open a document, WordPerfect creates a new document window for the document and puts the document into that window. You can then switch from one document window to another by selecting the one you want from the **W**indow menu. When you insert a document, it is retrieved into the current window at the cursor position (so, you can insert one document into another). Wow!

So How Do I Open a Document?

If you know the location and name of the file you want to open, it's easy. If you have no clue what the name is or where it's located, skip ahead to Lesson 14 to learn how to use the QuickFinder to help you.

To open a document, press **Ctrl+O**, or open the **F**ile menu and select **O**pen. (You can also click on the **Open** button on the Power Bar.) In the Open File dialog box that appears (see Figure 13.1), type the drive letter, path, and name of the file you want to open in the File**n**ame text box. Or click on your selections from the appropriate list boxes. Press **Enter**, or click on the **OK** button. WordPerfect opens a new document window and retrieves the specified document into the window. Incredible!

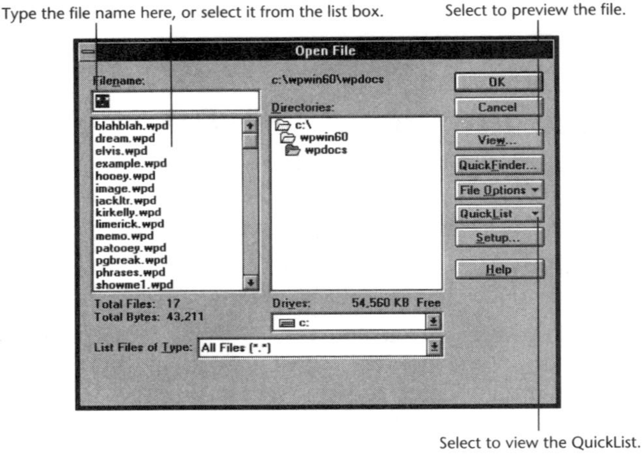

Figure 13.1 This is the Open File dialog box.

Tip

Starting with a Clean Slate Starting a document is easy. To open an empty document window, open the **F**ile menu, and select **N**ew. That's all there is to it. You can also press **Ctrl+N** or click on the **New Document** button on the Power Bar. This stuff is so easy!

Inserting a Document

To insert a document, first change to the document window in which you want to retrieve the document. Move the cursor where you want to insert the document. Then open the **I**nsert menu, and select F**i**le. The Insert File dialog box appears.

Type the drive letter, path, and name of the file you want to insert in the File**n**ame text box, or select it from the list box. Press **Enter**, or click on the **I**nsert button. A dialog box usually pops up, asking you if you want to insert the file into the current document. Select Yes, and Shazam! It's inserted.

Tip

A Snappy Comeback WordPerfect remembers the names and locations of the last four files you worked on and lets you open them directly from the **F**ile menu. How's that for convenience? To open one of these files, just open the **F**ile menu, and select the one you want from the bottom of the menu.

We're finished with this fetching business, so give yourself a couple of Scooby snacks, and let's move on. Next, you will learn how to print out your document so your coworkers won't think you've been playing Solitaire all day.

Lesssson 14

Quickly Finding Files with QuickFinder

The Find Feature Is All Well and Good, but I Need to Find a File, Not a Word

So, you've lost your files, eh? You've probably lost your marbles looking for them. (My own marbles hit the road years ago. Join the club.) Never fear, you can find those files with the QuickFinder. It's basically the lost and found department of WordPerfect for Windows.

First of all, you have to have some inkling of what it is you're looking for. Pretend that you made a file a few months ago and you can't remember what the name is or what the directory is, and you don't want to search through the hundreds of WordPerfect for Windows files you have saved. (You don't clean out your directories very often.) The only thing you can remember is that the file had the word "Blam" in it. With other word processors, this would be hopeless. They would laugh at you. Not WordPerfect for Windows. It says, "So, you can only remember one word, huh? Don't worry, it's no problem."

To use the QuickFinder, select QuickFinder from the File menu. There's also a button marked **QuickFinder** on some appropriate dialog boxes (like the Open File and Insert File dialog boxes) that you can select to go to the QuickFinder. The dialog box that appears looks like the one in Figure 14.1.

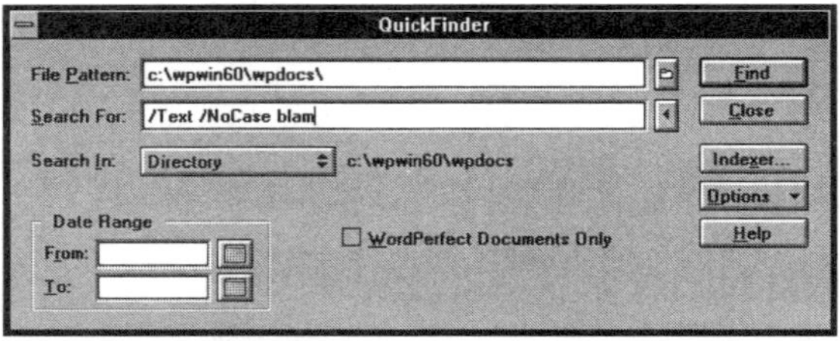

Figure 14.1 *The QuickFinder is WordPerfect's lost and found.*

In the File **P**attern text box, type in the directory you want to search. WordPerfect will search all the files in that directory. If you don't know the directory, leave *.* in the text box. Or click on the little button to the right of the text box, called the Browse button, and select a directory from the dialog box that pops up.

Okay, you've got the directory selected. Now here's where it gets tricky. You have to tell WordPerfect what to search for. You should use the drop-down menu that you get by clicking on the button to the right of the **S**earch For text box. It's shown in Figure 14.2.

See how the **S**earch For text box in the figure says **/Text**? That's because I selected **T**ext Only from the Document Components submenu. I also selected **N**ot Case Sensitive from the Case **S**ensitivity submenu because I don't know whether the word I'm looking for is capitalized. When you select these options, or *search parameters*, as I like to call them, they'll show up in the **S**earch For text box.

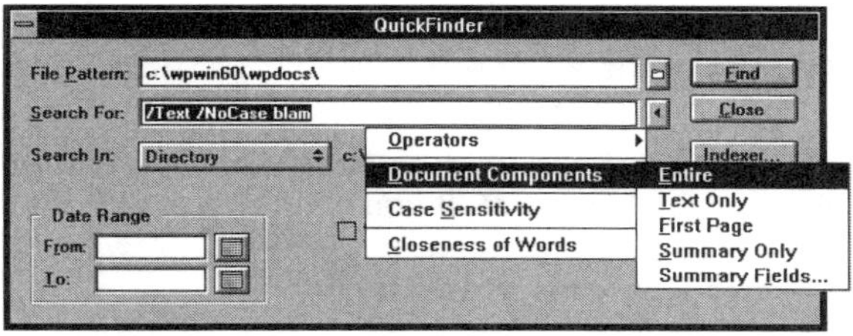

Figure 14.2 *Use this menu to specify the search parameters.*

Okay, we're just about ready to roll. All you have to do now is select the **Search For** text box, and then type in the word you want to search for. The word should appear after the search parameters. Now, select **Find**.

A dialog box will briefly appear on the screen, showing you which files WordPerfect is searching. When the search is finished, the Search Results List dialog box will appear (see Figure 14.3), and you'll see a list of the results. Amazing!

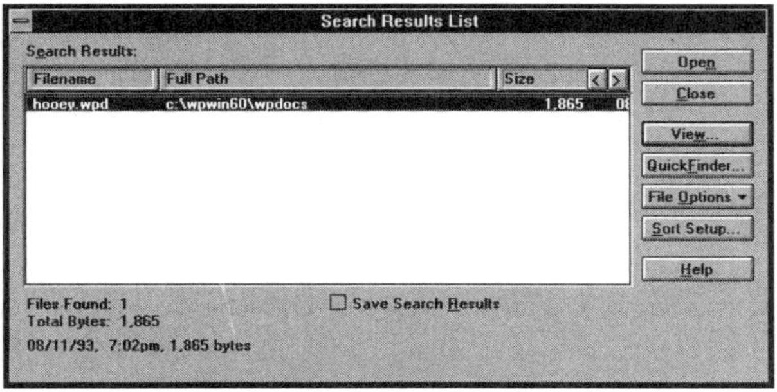

Figure 14.3 *This dialog box tells me that the word "blam" was found in the file named HOOEY.WPD.*

All you need to do now is select View if you want to preview the file or select Open if you want to open the file. And you thought this was going to be difficult.

The QuickFinder is actually a very cool tool once you get the hang of it. If you want to learn about the more advanced options associated with the QuickFinder, consult your manual.

Now that you've found your files, I'll teach you how to print them. Look on the next page.

Lesson 15

Can I Get That to Go? (Printing Your Document)

Before You Can Print, You Have to Select a Printer

If you have only one printer installed to run with Windows, you do not have to select a printer before you print. For you lucky ducks that have more than one printer, you may want to select another printer to use.

To select a printer, open the File menu, and select Select Printer. The Select Printer dialog box appears, as shown in Figure 15.1. Use the arrow keys to highlight the printer you want to use, and press **Enter** (or double-click on the name of the printer).

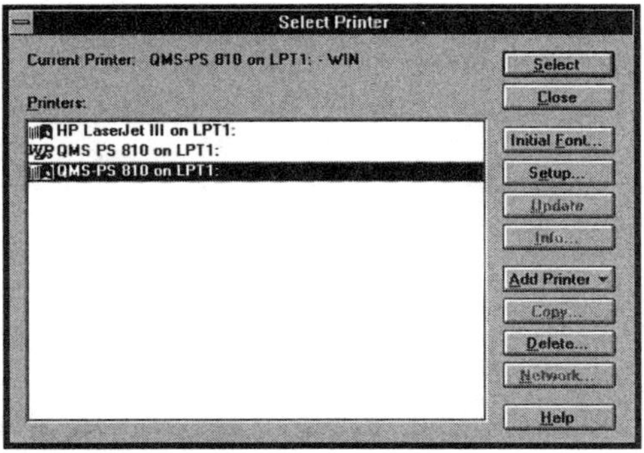

Figure 15.1 *Use the Select Printer dialog box to choose the printer you want to use.*

Tip

A Thousand Different Ways Of course, there's another way to get to the Select Printer dialog box. From the regular Print dialog box, choose the **S**elect button.

Can I Look at This Before I Print It?

It's usually a big help to see how your document will look in print before you actually print it. Weirdly enough, WordPerfect for Windows doesn't have an actual Print Preview feature like many word processors do. It does, however, have the Zoom feature. You can use it to see how the text will look on the page and how any graphic elements will appear in relation to the text.

To zoom in on your document, open the **V**iew menu, and select **Z**oom. In the Zoom dialog box that appears, select **F**ull Page, then select **OK**. The document appears in Full Page view on the screen, as shown in Figure 15.2.

Tip

Instant Zoom Click on the **Page Zoom Full** button on the Power Bar to see your full page quickly. You can also click on the **Page Zoom Full** button to get back to the regular page view when you're done previewing. But wait, there's more! You can select the regular **Zoom** button on the Power Bar and select the zoom percentage you want, or select **Full Page**. The fun never ends.

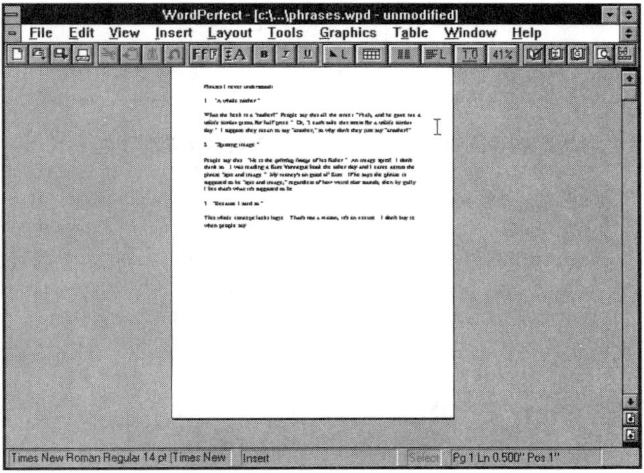

Figure 15.2 *Who's zooming who?*

To get back to the regular page view, select the **V**iew menu and **Z**oom command again. Then select **1**00% in the dialog box and select **OK**. Bam—normalcy.

Get to the Printing Already!

Okay, okay. You can either print a document that's currently active (it's open and the title bar is highlighted), or you can print a file that's already been saved. For sanity's sake, let's start with printing the active document.

It's a snap. Press **F5**, or open the **F**ile menu, and select **P**rint. (You can also click on the **Print** button on the Power Bar. As if you couldn't guess.) The Print dialog box appears. Select **F**ull Document under the Print Selection section, and then press **Enter** to select the Print button. WordPerfect prints one copy of your document. Are you happy now?

> **Why Isn't This Printing?** If your printer does not start printing, make sure your printer is on, has paper, and is on-line, or lined up correctly. (Most printers have a light that shows when the printer is on-line.) If that doesn't work, then you've obviously done something very strange and obscure, and you'll have to check your printer's documentation to figure it out.

This Isn't What I Want

The last section just told you the basics in no-frills printing. However, the Print dialog box offers several wonderful options that you can fiddle around with to tell WordPerfect to print a document in a special way. Let's look at them, shall we? First, press **F5** (or select **F**ile **P**rint) to open the Print dialog box.

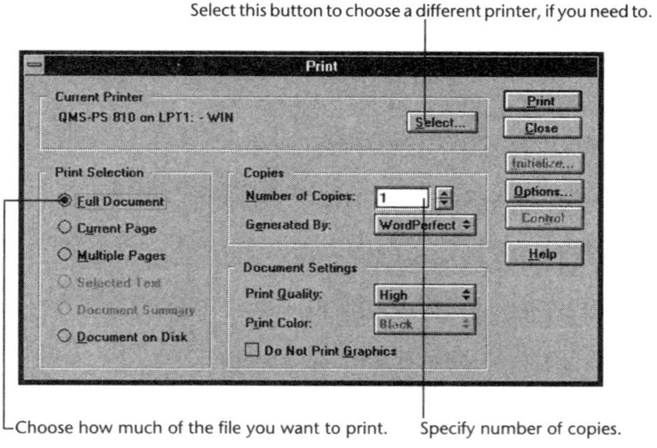

Figure 15.3 *The Print dialog box.*

Just look at all the fun we can have with this dialog box. You can tell WordPerfect to print only the current page, or you can select **M**ultiple Pages. In that case, you'll get a dialog box called, surprisingly enough, Multiple Pages, in which you can specify the pages you want to print. (You have to type the numbers in numerical order. Otherwise, WordPerfect gets confused.) Refer to Table 15.1 if you want to know how to type in the page numbers so WordPerfect will know what to print.

Table 15.1 Typing in Page Numbers

Type this . . .	To print this
2	Page 2
2 4	Pages 2 and 4
2,4,6	Pages 2, 4, and 6
2–4	Pages 2 through 4
2–	Page 2 to the end of the document
–4	From the beginning of the document through page 4
2–4 6	Pages 2 through 4 and page 6

In the Print Selection section, you can also choose to print some text that you've previously selected. Notice that there is also an option called Document on Disk. We'll talk about that later. Let's move on.

In the Copies section, you can type in the number of copies you want to print in the Number of Copies text box. You can also use the spin buttons to specify a number.

There's an option called Generated By, which you can use to toggle between the choices *WordPerfect* and *Printer*. If you are using WordPerfect to generate three copies, WordPerfect will send three complete copies to the printer, one-by-one. If you tell your printer to generate three copies, it will print three copies of page 1, then three copies of page 2, and so on.

You can use the Document Settings section to change the Print Quality. For the final product, you'll probably want to keep this on High. But you can change it to Draft or some other setting if the print quality doesn't matter.

If you have a color printer, you can specify the Print Color in the Document Settings section. You can also tell WordPerfect not to print graphics (if you have any) by selecting the Do Not Print Graphics check box.

If you want to choose even more options, choose the Options button. You'll get a new dialog box in which you'll be able to do things like change the print order from forward to reverse. When you're done fooling around in these dialog boxes, choose Print. Your file will print as you specified.

What if the File I Want to Print Is Not Currently Active?

Say you are currently slaving away in one file, and then you realize that you need to refer to some information in another file. Aiee! What should you do? Well, a good idea is to print out the other file so you can look at both files at the same time: one on the screen and one on paper.

Fortunately, you can do this with very little hassle in WordPerfect for Windows. First, press **F5**, or select File Print. Under Print Selection in the Print dialog box, choose **Document on Disk**. Then, select the Print button. The Document on Disk dialog box will pop up, as shown in Figure 15.4.

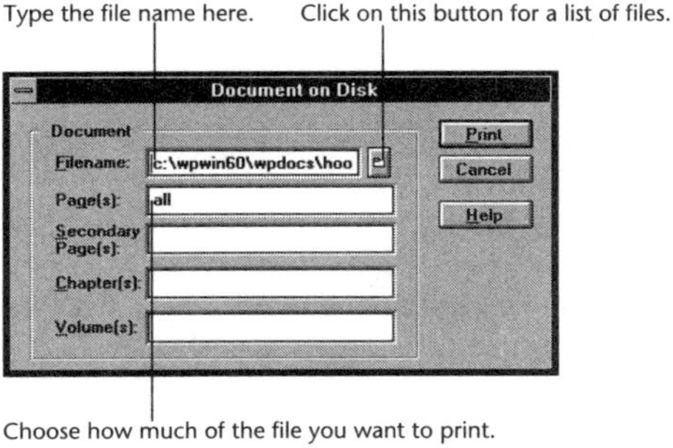

Figure 15.4 *Pick the file you want to print from the Document on Disk dialog box.*

In the **Filename** text box, type the path and file name of the file you want to print. (If you don't know the path, click on the little icon next to the text box. It'll show you a list of files you can select.) Specify the pages you want to print in the **Pages** text box, if you only want to print certain pages. Otherwise, WordPerfect will print the whole document. Select **Print**, and the document will print.

Now you know how to print out your files so your coworkers won't think you've been sitting around twirling your thumbs. In the next lesson, you'll learn about those pesky WordPerfect codes. Just what you wanted to know, huh?

Lesson 16

These Codes Are a Little Revealing

What Are WordPerfect Codes?

Whenever you do anything to your document like press **Tab** or **Enter**, or make text bold, WordPerfect inserts a code. Most codes appear two times—the first one turns on the attribute and the other turns it off. (A text *attribute* is a characteristic that makes it special, like bold or italics.) These codes work in the background to control the appearance of your text. WordPerfect adds the following three types of codes to documents:

- **Paired codes** Codes used for turning an attribute on and off are called paired codes because WordPerfect always inserts two codes. It's like a pair of shoes. One doesn't do you much good unless you have the other one.
- **Open codes** Open codes (such as codes that control the left and right margins) control the text from the current position of the code up to the next open code that changes the same format setting, or to the end of the document.
- **Single codes** Unlike open codes that control formatting from the current position forward, single codes act only at the current position. For example, when you press the Enter key at the end of a paragraph, WordPerfect inserts a hard return code.

Normally, you don't have to think about the codes; they do their work in the background. However, if your text looks funny on-screen or in print, or if your margins are not turning out as expected, you can view the codes to find the cause of the problem and correct it. Hold onto your hat, Sherlock.

Deciphering Your Codes Without Using a Secret Decoder Ring

You're probably wondering what these codes look like, right? To view the codes, you can display the Reveal Codes screen shown in Figure 16.1. To turn Reveal Codes on or off, you can press **Alt+F3**. Or you can open the **View** menu and select Reveal **C**odes.

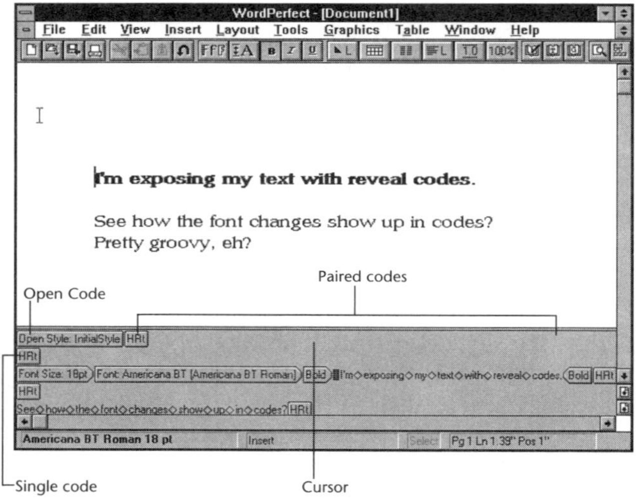

Figure 16.1 The Reveal Codes screen shows you the codes that control your text.

When you have Reveal Codes on, the screen splits in two. Normal text appears in the top part of the screen, and the text with codes appears in the lower half. See how a lot of them look like little sales tags? Those are the paired codes. They point in the direction of the code that matches. The rectangular codes are single or open codes. The cursor appears in this part of the screen as a black rectangle. You can type, edit, and format your document as you normally would, but now you can work with the codes as well. The excitement never ends around here.

This @$*!& Code Is Wrong!

If the codes are wrong and they're throwing your document off, you can edit them. In most cases, editing consists of deleting the code. For example, if you want to unbold some text, you can delete the **Bold** codes. To delete a code, point to it with your mouse then drag it off the Reveal Codes part of the screen, like in Figure 16.2. (In other words, drag it toward the document.) You'll see a blank space that looks like a hole where the code used to be, then when you release the mouse button . . . Blip! The code will be deleted.

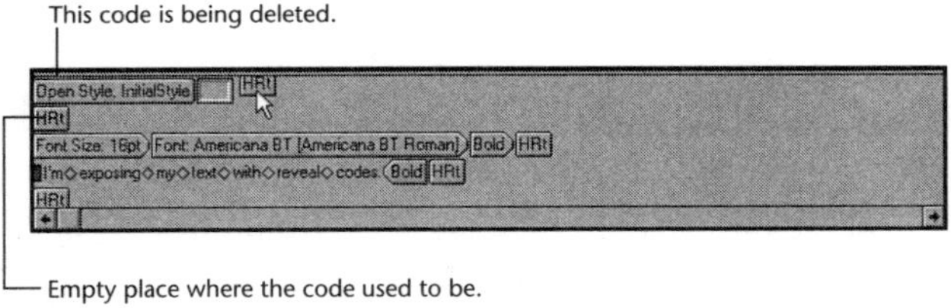

Figure 16.2 *I'm deleting this little guy because I have too many hard returns here.*

If you want to delete a paired code, drag either code off the Reveal Codes part of the screen. Both codes are automatically deleted. I hope you're keeping track of all this.

A good way to adjust open code settings is to move the cursor just past the code, change the setting as you normally would, and then delete the old code.

Whenever you enter a format setting that inserts an open code in your document, WordPerfect automatically inserts the code at the most logical place in the document. For example, if you change the margins for a paragraph, WordPerfect inserts the code at the beginning of the paragraph, replacing any Left/Right Margin code that might already exist.

I Don't Like the Way My Codes Look

If the Reveal Codes screen is so ugly that it gets on your nerves, you can change it. Select Preferences from the File menu, and then select the Display icon. In the Display Preferences dialog box (Figure 16.3), select the Reveal Codes option button, and the bottom part of the dialog box will transform into options specifically designated for the Reveal Codes option.

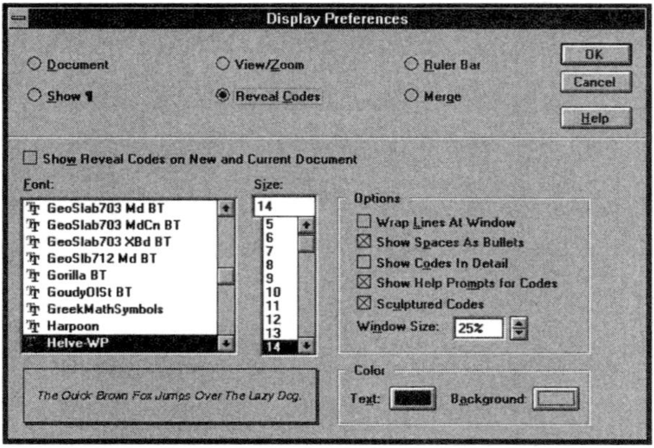

Figure 16.3 *If the codes are too ugly to look at, change the way they look with this dialog box.*

Change whatever you want. You can change the typeface and the font size, the color of the text and background, the way the codes themselves are displayed, and so on. When you're finished, select **OK**, and then close the Preferences dialog box.

A final word of warning about Reveal Codes: if you've got the Power Bar, the Button Bar, and the Ruler Bar on when you turn on Reveal Codes, you'll have about a half an inch of space for your document. It's not necessary to leave this option on all the time. Just use it when you need it. On that note, let's move on to our next subject: tab settings.

Lesson 17

Slaving over Tab Settings

Why Do I Have to Worry About Tabs?

Tabs are a very touchy subject for me; I've had more than my share of tab trauma. They remind me of this nasty, old English professor I had in college. Big as an ox but didn't smell quite as nice. Anyway, I got along with her fine until I realized that no matter how good an essay I thought I wrote, she always found a way to dig into it and mess it up. Tabs usually behave that way when I'm doing something important, like making a table. You get one of those suckers wrong and it throws the whole thing off. It's as if the tab gods, like my English professor, have it in for me.

Don't worry, tabs aren't really that difficult. I just happen to be cursed. I don't think it's contagious. See, whenever you press the **Tab** key in a document, WordPerfect moves the cursor (and any text that's to the right of the cursor) to a *tab stop*. Unless you specify otherwise, tab stops are set at half-inch intervals from the left margin. So, if you press the Tab key once, the cursor moves one-half inch in from the left margin. This is basic stuff. Let's move on.

I Hate These Tab Stop Settings

Initially, all tab stops are left tab stops. Those are the ones that make your text flush left. You don't have to put up with that if you don't want to; you can center the text, right-align it, or align a decimal point on the tab stop. Figure 17.1 shows the various types of tab stops and how you might use them.

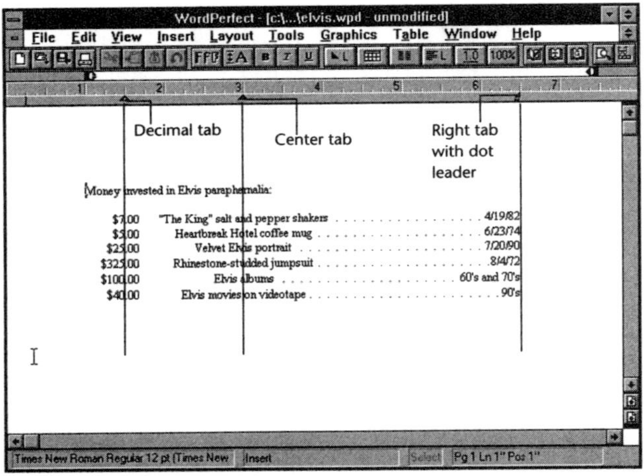

Figure 17.1 *Text aligns differently depending on the type of tab stop.*

To set the tab settings, first move the cursor to the appropriate place. This can be anywhere inside the paragraph whose tab stop settings you want to clear or at the start of a new paragraph. You can also highlight a section of text, if you want. Now, you can do one of two things: you can use the menu bar or the QuickMenu (as shown in Figure 17.2).

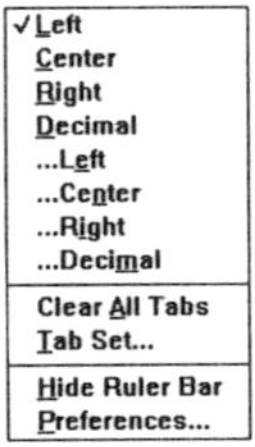

Figure 17.2 *The QuickMenu for tab settings.*

I prefer to use the QuickMenu. The menu bar thing turns into a big mess, and it confuses me. I already have enough trouble with tabs, so I'm going to take the path with the least hassle. Using the keyboard to set tabs is a huge pain in the neck, and I don't want to burden you with that. It's a bit cumbersome. If you don't have a mouse and you have to use the keyboard, please refer to your manual. Otherwise, use the mouse at all times.

> **Tip**
>
> **No Pain, No Gain** If you want to learn how to use the menu bar, this will get you started: select **L**ine from the **L**ayout menu, and then choose **T**ab Set. You'll get a dialog box that lets you do the same things I'm going to talk about in this lesson, plus a few more advanced things.

If you've forgotten what a QuickMenu is, listen to this: did you ever notice that your mouse has two buttons and that you only use the right mouse button once in a blue moon? You get a chance to use it when you use a QuickMenu. Point at the very bottom part of the Ruler Bar (What? You haven't turned it on yet? Turn it on!), and click with the right mouse button. Choose whatever you want from the menu. (You can also use the **Tab Set** button on the Power Bar. It does basically the same thing.)

> **Tip**
>
> **Hey, This Doesn't Look Like the One in the Figure** If your QuickMenu has things like Paragraph Format and Margins on it, then you clicked on the wrong part of the Ruler Bar. Throughout this lesson,
>
> *continues*

continued

when I say, "Click on the Ruler Bar," I mean the very bottom where the triangles are. If you're clicking where the inch increments are, you're doing it wrong.

You can choose from the regular Left, Center, Right, and Decimal options, but there are also dot leader options that we haven't talked about yet. Those are basically the same except that they put dots between the tab stops, like in a table of contents or something. Those can be cool if you have a need for that kind of thing.

How Do I Add New Tab Stops?

You can add tab stop settings to the tab ruler at any point in the document. First, you have to move the cursor anywhere inside the paragraph whose tab stops you want to set, or start a new paragraph. Then, bring up the QuickMenu by clicking the right mouse button in the Ruler Bar.

Select the type of tab you want. Now, just click the place on the Ruler Bar where you want the tab. Presto! If you want to add a different type of tab in another place, call up the QuickMenu again, and click on the new type. Then click on the place for the new tab. This is so easy!

How Do I Get Rid of These Blasted Things?!

The Ruler Bar can get cluttered with the various tab stop settings. If you need to use only two or three tab stop settings, you may want to clear some. That way, you don't have to press the Tab key several times to move to the desired tab stop.

To get rid of everything, select Clear All Tabs from the QuickMenu. Zap. A clean slate. Now you can add whatever tabs you want. If you only need to delete a couple of tab settings, drag them off the Ruler Bar. (Just point at the offending tab triangle, and drag it onto the document part of the screen.)

Tip

What's the Best Way, in Your Opinion? If I'm going to be doing something that's fairly tab-heavy, I usually like to clear all the tabs first, and then set my own where I want them. No Ruler Bar is going to dictate where I set my tabs, that's for sure. I'll do it my way.

There Are Some Weird Hidden Codes for These, Aren't There?

Of course, there is a weird hidden code for the tab settings. Whenever you change the tab stop settings, WordPerfect inserts a code at the place where the tab occurs (See Figure 17.3.) There is also a code at the beginning of the paragraph (or whatever is affected) that tells WordPerfect where the tabs are set. To return the tab stops to the original settings, display the Reveal Codes screen, and delete the tab code at the beginning of the paragraph (or whatever is affected). Your tabs will all change to left tabs.

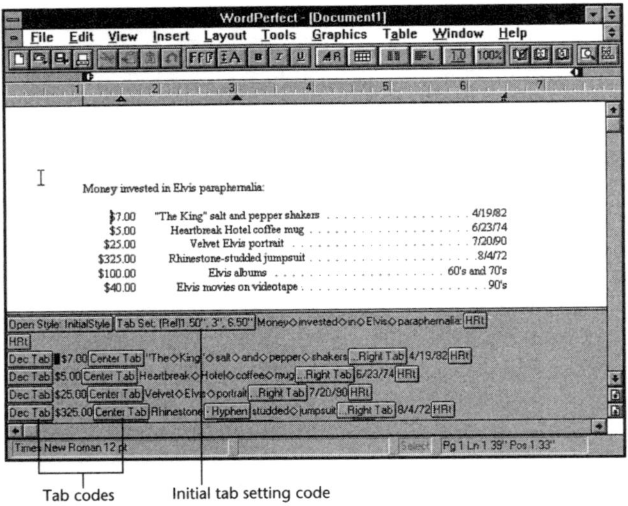

Figure 17.3 *Some pesky codes crop up for tab settings, too*

Enough of the tabs already. Let me tell you about alignment and line spacing.

Lesson 18

Spaced Out and Justified

Wordsworth Never Had It So Easy

Not to load you up with college anecdotes, but I have one that actually fits here. Remember when your professor wanted ten pages on some twelve-line poem by William Wordsworth? No way you could squeeze ten pages out of that thing, so if you were anything like me, you made the margins really big and adjusted the line spacing to the highest it could go. (I also made the size of the type larger. I'm one of those people who always pushes the limits.) You might have also messed around with making big indents or changing the alignment of your text. If you did, you were a lot like me.

So How Do I Change the Margins?

Ah, I can tell the wheels are turning in your head now. Dreaming of fitting your entire history onto a one-page resume? Hoping to stretch that measly one-page report into three? If you want to do these things, you'll have to change the margin setting from WordPerfect's default, which is one inch all the way around.

First, press **Ctrl+Home** to move the cursor to the top of the document. The Margin codes affect all text from the beginning of the document to the end, or up to the next Margin code. Press **Ctrl+F8**, or open the Layout menu and select **Margins**. The Margin Format dialog box appears, as shown in Figure 18.1.

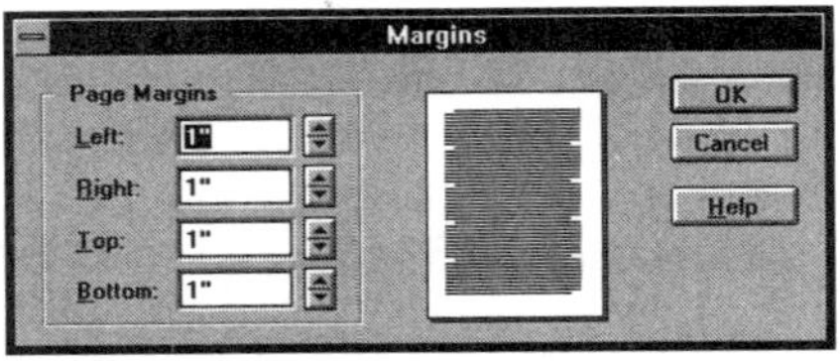

Figure 18.1 *The Margins dialog box.*

To change the left, right, top, or bottom margin, select the margin you want to change, type the new setting (in inches), and press **Enter**. You can also use the spin buttons, if you want. This is utter simplicity.

Tip

Marginal Changes If you only want to change the margins for certain text, like one paragraph, highlight it before you change the margins. Only the selected text will be affected.

The Bold, the Beautiful, the Justified

In the last lesson, you learned a little bit about justification when you learned about Left, Center, and Right Tabs. This is generally the same concept, but you're aligning whole paragraphs instead of one tab stop.

All you have to do to change the justification (or *alignment*, as some call it), is position the cursor, and then choose Justification from the Layout menu. (You can also click on the **Justification** button on the Power Bar.) Select the option you want from the submenu. You can choose Left, Right, Center, Full, or All. (The All option justifies *everything*, including the last sentence in the paragraph, which might look weird if you only have a couple of words on the line.) See some examples of the different justification styles in Figure 18.2.

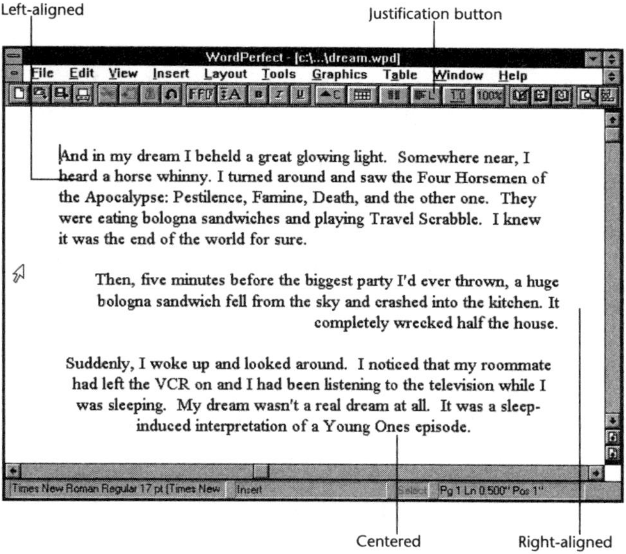

Figure 18.2 *Left, right, and center justification.*

> **Tip**
>
> **Where Should I Put the Cursor?** All text after the cursor position will be affected, so be careful when you place your cursor. If you only want to change the alignment of a specific amount of text, highlight it. Only the selected text will be affected.

Put a Dent in Your Text

To indent paragraphs from the left or right margin, first position your cursor in the paragraph you want to indent. (The indent only affects one paragraph, so if you want more than that, you have to highlight what you want.) Then, select Paragraph from the Layout menu. Select the type of indent you want from the submenu that appears. Here's the low-down on what they do:

- **Indent** This is a regular indent. It only indents the left margin. The shortcut key is F7.
- **Hanging Indent** This indents all of the paragraph except the first line. You would probably use this in a bibliography, or something like that. The shortcut key combination is Ctrl+F7.
- **Double Indent** This indents the left and right margins of the paragraph. Use this for long quotations in text. The shortcut key combination is Ctrl+Shift+F7.
- **Back Tab** This is sort of like a hanging indent, except that it pushes the first line to the left of the margin, instead of pushing the text to the right. It looks like a hanging indent, but it's over farther to the left. There is no shortcut key for this one. Bummer.

If you have some really tricky things to do to your paragraph, use the Paragraph Format dialog box, as shown in Figure 18.3. You can get it by selecting Format from the Paragraph submenu of the Layout menu. You can make specific adjustments in this dialog box.

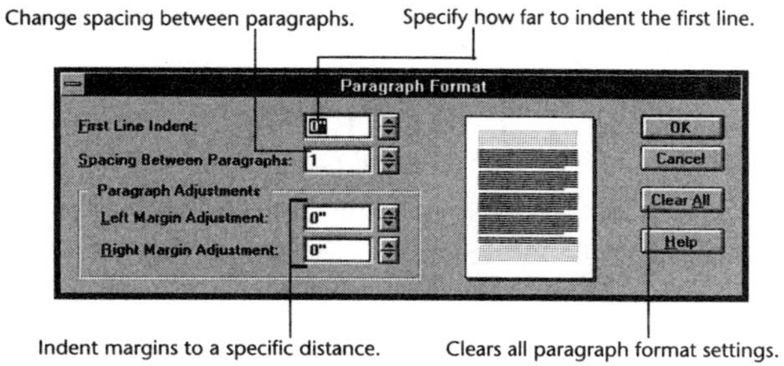

Figure 18.3 *The infamous Paragraph Format dialog box.*

Tip

Isn't There a Shortcut? No, not really. You can do a fast regular indent by using the **I**ndent command from the QuickMenu that pops up when you right click anywhere in the paragraph. But for anything else, you have to do some real work.

About That Line Spacing You Mentioned . . .

If you want to scrunch things together or spread them out, a good way to accomplish this is to change the line spacing. WordPerfect single-spaces the text, so no extra space is inserted between each line of text, but you can change it. For example, you may want to change to triple-spacing so you can write comments on your paper.

You can change the line spacing for an entire document or a section of it; move the cursor anywhere in the document where you want to start the line spacing change. Open the Layout menu, and select Line. From the submenu that appears, select Spacing.

A dialog box will show up, letting you enter the amount of spacing you want. Type in the appropriate number or use the spin buttons, then select **OK**. Everything after your cursor will be affected. Unless, of course, you change the line spacing later on in your document. In that case, everything between the two codes (remember those?) will be affected.

A much easier way to select the line spacing is to use the **Line Spacing** button on the Power Bar. Gee, that thing really speeds things up, doesn't it? I mean, I've mentioned it at least four or five times in the past three lessons. Those WordPerfect folks really outdid themselves this time.

In this lesson, you learned that I was a sneaky college student, and you learned how to become equally sneaky by changing margin settings, line spacing, and other nifty things. Next, you'll learn more tricks for making the text appear as you want it. Step this way!

Lesson 19

That Look Is All Wrong for Your Text

What Are Fonts?

Fonts are used in your document to change the way your text looks. A *font* is any set of characters that has the same *typeface* and *type size*. For example, Palatino 10-point is a font. Palatino is the typeface, and 10-point is the size.

Tip

Trivial Point There are almost exactly 72 *points* in an inch, by the way. I thought I'd tell you in case it pops up in a big Trivial Pursuit game.

The font *style* is something like bold, underline, italic, and so on. It's also called *character formatting* or *character enhancement*, or whatever the current buzzword is. Style is like those little people (read: plastic sticks with knobs on the top) you get to put in your car in the game *Life*. You can pick which "style" you want, blue or pink, but they're all stuck riding in the same car. With a font, you can choose any style you want, but it's all the same typeface.

In WordPerfect for Windows, you can change fonts at three levels. First, you can change the *setup initial font* to specify which font you want WordPerfect for Windows to use for all new documents. Second, if you start a new document and you don't want to use the setup initial font for the document, you can override the setup initial font by specifying a *document initial font.* Third, you can then override the document initial font within a document by specifying a font for a single letter, word, heading, or other text block. Too complicated for you?

Just One Font for Me, I Don't Want to Spoil My Dinner

To change the setup initial font or the document initial font, press **F9**, or open the **Layout** menu and select **Font**. When the Font dialog box appears, select the **Initial Font** box. The Document Initial Font dialog box appears, as shown in Figure 19.1.

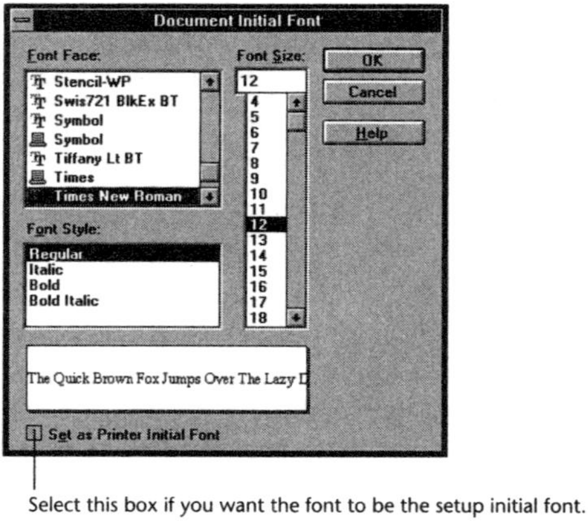

Figure 19.1 *The Document Initial Font dialog box lets you select a font to be used for the entire document.*

Choose any of the settings you want. You can change the typeface, the size, and the style of the font. What flexibility! If you want this font to be the setup initial font, select the **Set as Printer Initial Font** check box at the bottom of the dialog box. If you do that, this font will be used automatically for every new document you open. If you don't select the check box, the font will only be in effect for the current document.

Tip

Someone, Give Me a Clue If you're not sure what font you'll be using when you start a document, check the status bar. The current font is always displayed there. You want another clue? It was Colonel Mustard with the wrench in the Conservatory.

Live a Little, Change a Font

If you want to override the document initial font (or the setup initial font, for that matter) for a certain block of text, you can choose a new font. First, select the text you want to change. Then, press **F9**, or open the **Layout** menu and select **Font**. The **Font** dialog box appears, as shown in Figure 19.2.

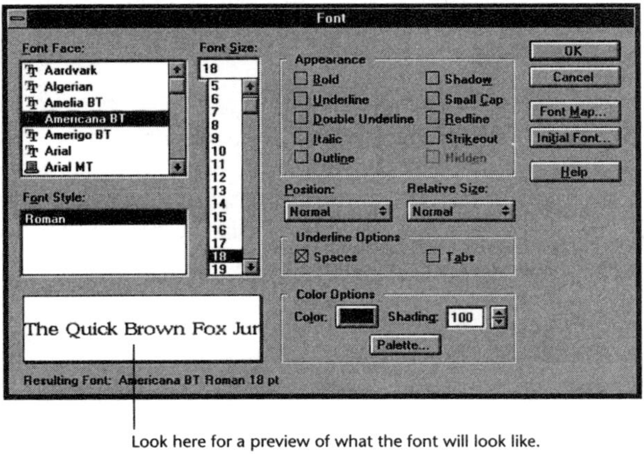

Figure 19.2 *The Font dialog box lets you specify the font to use for the selected text.*

Wow! Look at all this stuff you can change! You can use a different typeface, a new size, a different color, whatever you want. Whenever you change something, an example of it shows up in the Sample box. How helpful. That way you can see what you get before you get it. Some people call that particular feature WYSBYGI (What-You-See-Before-You-Get-It), which is pronounced "Whiz-Biggie." Granted, the people who use that term are probably a little on the soft-headed side, but at least you'll know what it means if you hear it.

When you're done making all your changes, select the **OK** button. The text in your document will be changed, and you're ready to roll. (Let's hope you get doubles.)

Tip

Someone, Give Me a Shortcut Here's a surprise: look on the Power Bar for tools to change the typeface and size of your font. If you didn't see that one coming, go directly to jail. Do not pass Go. Do not collect $200.

Now you've learned all about fonts and how to make them appear as you want. Next, you will learn how to use headers and footers. Stop frowning! Sure, they're not as fun as, say, a board game, but they're not that bad.

Lesson 20

Hassle-Free Headers and Footers

Creating a Header or Footer

Headers are those things that appear at the top of every page of a document. Footers, appropriately, appear at the bottom of every page. To create a header or footer, move the cursor to the first page on which you want the header or footer to appear. (The header or footer will appear on this and all following pages.)

To create one, open the Layout menu and select Header/Footer. When the Headers/Footers dialog box appears, select whichever one you want. If this is your first, it's probably a good idea to select A. Then, select Create.

The Header or Footer edit screen appears, as shown in Figure 20.1. This screen looks like the normal edit screen, except the Header/Footer Feature Bar has appeared.

Type the text that you want to use for the header or footer. You can type up to one page of text, but usually (just so you know) you type only one or two lines. You can have WordPerfect for Windows insert things like the page number, the date, or the file name. To have WordPerfect insert the page number in the header or footer, move the cursor where you want the page number to be inserted, and select Page Number from the Number button in the Feature Bar. You can use the Insert menu, like usual, to insert the date and file name.

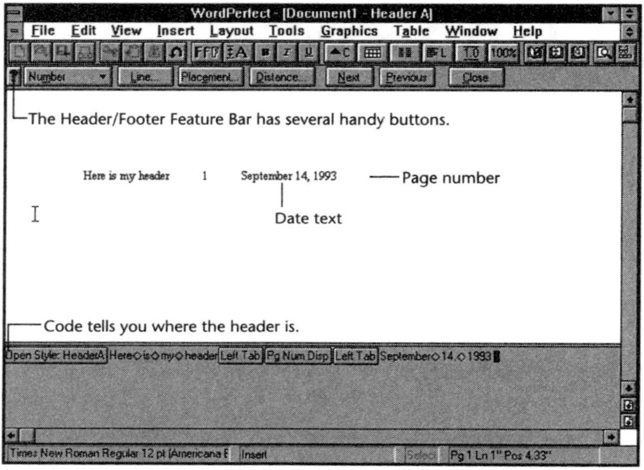

Figure 20.1 *A sample header complete with date and page number (Reveal Codes is turned on).*

You can also press **Ctrl+D** to insert Date Text or **Ctrl+Shift+D** to insert the Date Code. If you choose Date Text, WordPerfect for Windows will automatically insert today's date and it won't change. If you choose Date Code, a code will be inserted telling WordPerfect to insert today's date. With that option, the date on your paper changes when the actual date changes. If you print it tomorrow, you'll get tomorrow's date.

When you finish entering your header or footer, select the Close button to exit the screen. You can also click anywhere outside of the header/footer area to return to your document.

Tip

Hey—I Can't See My Header/Footer! Headers and footers are not displayed in Draft view. If you want to see them, switch to either Page view or Two Page view. Press **Alt+F5** to quickly go to Page view.

A Head by a Foot: Editing a Header or Footer

If you decide to change your header or footer later, you can edit it by selecting Header/Footer from the Layout menu and then selecting the one you want to edit from the list. Choose the Edit button. (You can achieve the same end by clicking anywhere in the header/footer area.) The Header or Footer edit screen appears, showing you the text you previously typed for this header or footer. You can edit the header or footer as you would edit any text.

Tip

Burning at Both Ends If you want something to appear flush left (like the date) and something else to appear flush right (like the page number) in your header or footer, use Header A for one and Header B for the other.

Tell Me More about This Feature Bar

First of all, you can display the Feature Bar at any time by clicking in the header/footer area, then clicking the right mouse button and selecting Feature Bar from the QuickMenu. Here's what you can do with it:

- Number   Inserts a number in the header/footer; usually a page number unless you're doing something really advanced.
- Line   Inserts a line beneath your header or above your footer. Use the Create Graphic Line dialog box (as shown in Figure 20.2) to specify the type of line you want.

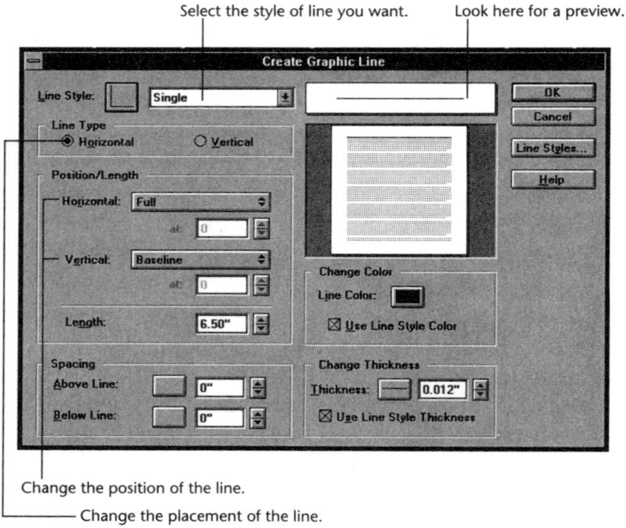

Figure 20.2 The Create Graphic Line dialog box.

- Placement   Lets you specify whether you want the header/footer to print on **O**dd Pages, **E**ven Pages, or Ever**y** Page. The default is Every Page.
- **D**istance   Lets you tell WordPerfect how much space to put between the header/footer and the text.

- Next and Previous These buttons let you go to the next or previous header/footer in the document.

Can I Turn This Off for Just One Page?

WordPerfect sets the header or footer on all the pages, the odd pages, or the even pages, according to your instructions. However, you may have a title page on which you do not want the header or footer to appear.

To turn a header or footer off for a single page, first move the cursor to the page for which you want to turn the header or footer off. Select Page from the Layout menu, and then select Suppress from the submenu. When the dialog box appears, select the one you want to turn off. Select OK. The specified header or footer will not appear on the current page.

In this lesson, you learned about those things at the top and bottom of pages. We're not finished with pages yet, though. Now I'll show you how to control the page divisions in a document and another way to number pages. Aren't I good to you?

Lesson 21

Breaking Pages and Controlling Numbers

Forcing a Page Break

When you're typing a document, WordPerfect automatically divides the document into pages based on the default page length and margin settings or on the settings you entered. Whenever WordPerfect determines that a new page should start, WordPerfect inserts a **SPg** code, which indicates a soft page break. It is automatically created by WordPerfect and is not permanent. It changes whenever you delete or add text. WordPerfect displays a black and gray horizontal line showing the page break on-screen.

Sometimes, you want to divide the text into pages yourself. For example, you may create a large table that you want to appear on a page by itself. In such a case, you can insert a *hard page break* in the document by moving the cursor where you want to create a page break and pressing **Ctrl+Enter**. WordPerfect inserts a **HPg** code at the cursor position and displays the page break as a black and gray horizontal line (see Figure 21.1).

Tip

You're Lying—It Does Not Look Like That Well, it doesn't look like a black and gray line if you're in Draft view, smarty-pants. In Draft view, a soft page break is shown as a horizontal line, and a hard page break is shown as a double horizontal line. Change to Page view to see things my way. So there.

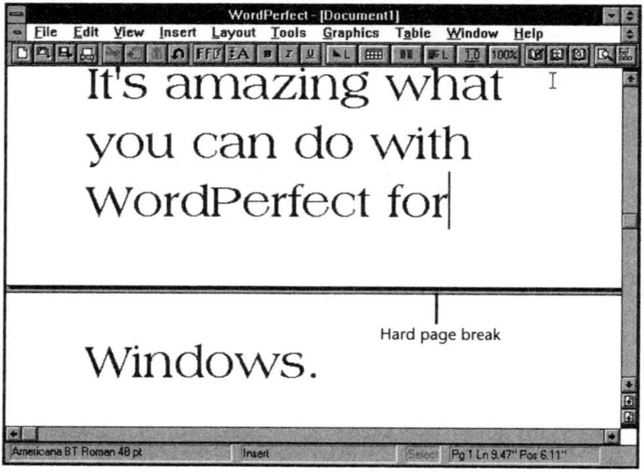

Figure 21.1 *A page break appears as a black and gray horizontal line.*

To remove a hard page break, press **Alt+F3** to turn on Reveal Codes, and delete the **HPg** code. You can also position the cursor at the beginning of the line following the page break and press **Backspace**.

Take a Number, Please

In Lesson 20, you learned how to add headers and footers to your document and how to insert a code in a header or footer that automatically inserts the correct page number. However, WordPerfect for Windows offers an easier way to number pages. (Oh, sure, now you tell us.)

First, press **Ctrl+Home** to move the cursor to the top of the document. Open the Layout menu, select Page, and then select Numbering from the submenu. The Page Numbering dialog box appears, as shown in Figure 21.2.

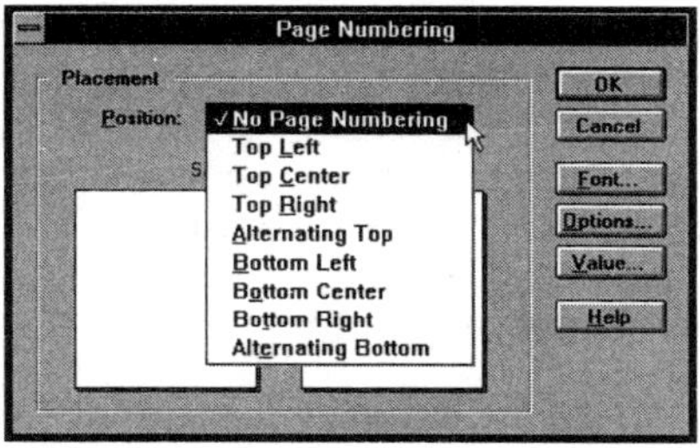

Figure 21.2 *Tell WordPerfect where you want it to put the page number in the Page Numbering dialog box.*

Under Position, specify where you want the page numbers placed on the page. Then press **Enter**, or select **OK**. If needed, select one of the buttons on the right of the dialog box.

The Options button brings up a dialog box that enables you to specify the numbering method you want to use (numbers, letters, or roman numerals). Tell it which one you want, and then select **OK**.

The Font button brings up the Page Numbering Font dialog box, which lets you change the font of the page number. You can make it something really classy or really illegible, whichever you want. Select **OK** when you're done messing up . . .er, I mean, putting the finishing touches on your font.

The Value button leads you to a dialog box where you can choose, among several other things, which number you want to start the page numbering with. Change the number in the New Page Number text box. Leave all other things alone unless you know what you're doing. Select **OK** when you're done.

In this lesson, you learned how to force a page break in a document (without using a crowbar) and how to use WordPerfect's page numbering feature (without using your fingers and toes). Next, you'll learn how to check your document for those unsightly spelling errors and blemishes (without using over-the-counter medication).

Lesson 22

Sumtimes I Don't Right Real Good

Checking Your Spelling with Speller

WordPerfect for Windows is equipped with a program that can check your document for spelling errors that your brain was obviously not equipped to handle. This amazing tool also checks for repeated words and capitalization errors. You can check a single word or page of the entire document or from the cursor position to the end of the document.

To check the spelling of a single word or page, or to check it from where the cursor is located to the end of the document, move the cursor where you want the spell checker to start. (If you want to check the entire document, the cursor can be anywhere.) Then, open the Tools menu, and select **S**peller. You can also click on the **Speller** button on the Power Bar. The Speller dialog box appears, as shown in Figure 22.1

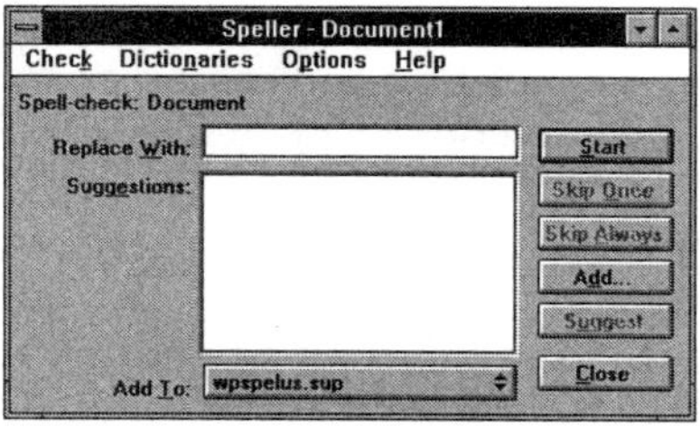

Figure 22.1 *Here's the dialog box you get when you select the Speller.*

Tell the Speller what to check by selecting an option from the Check menu. Select the Start button, to begin the search for spelling errors. If a word is found that does not match a word in its dictionary, WordPerfect displays the offending word in the Replace With text box, as shown in Figure 22.2.

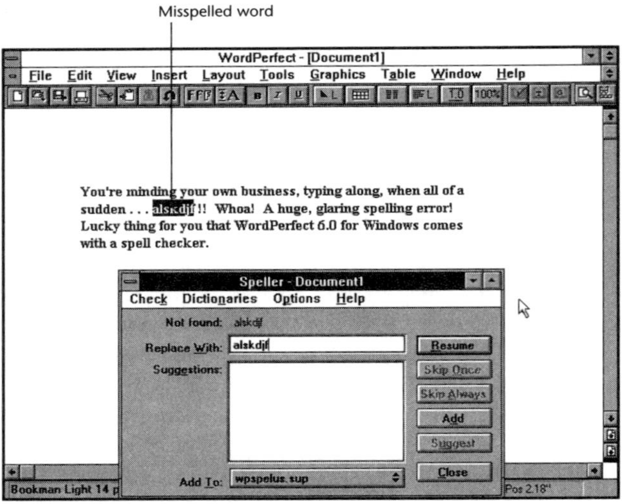

Figure 22.2 *Here's the little troublemaker.*

If WordPerfect finds a questionable word, take one of the following actions:

- Highlight the correct spelling in the Suggestions list, and choose Replace.
- To ignore the word and move on, select Skip Once (to ignore only this occurrence of the word) or Skip Always (to ignore every occurrence of this word).

- To add the word to WordPerfect's dictionary (so WordPerfect will never question it again), select A**d**d.
- To get more suggestions, select the S**u**ggest button.

Continue choosing things until WordPerfect displays a dialog box showing that the spell check is complete. Select **Y**es to close the Speller.

Tip

The Spell Checker Isn't Foolproof WordPerfect questions only those words that do not match a word in the spell checker's dictionary. If you type "to" when you mean to type "too," WordPerfect skips over the error. Sorry.

Since Speller is the tool you'll probably use the most often, that's the only tool I'm going to cover here. If you're feeling experimental, try out two other nifty tools: Grammatik (checks grammar) and Thesaurus (provides alternate word ideas). Check with your WordPerfect manual or with on-line Help if you need some assistance with these more advanced tools.

Guess What? This is the end! I've run out of things to say. Go and create lovely documents.

Appendix A

Installation Instructions

How Do I Install WordPerfect 6.0 for Windows?

First of all, you have to be in Windows. If you aren't, type **win** at the DOS prompt. You should see the beginning Program Manager screen.

From the File menu, select the **Run** command. Put the WordPerfect for Windows Install Disk 1 in the drive (drive A or drive B, depending upon which size disk you have). In the text box of the Run dialog box, type the appropriate drive letter and a colon, immediately followed by the word *install*. For example, if your disk is in drive A, you would type **A:INSTALL**.

Dialog boxes will pop up and ask you for information. In the first one, type your name and registration number, then choose Continue. In the second one, choose the Standard button so the regular WordPerfect program will be installed. (You can check with your documentation if you don't have enough disk space to install all the WordPerfect files. You can install a minimum configuration that doesn't take up as much space.)

Follow along with the dialog boxes. One will ask you to specify the drive to install the files on (choose your hard drive). The printer will show up in the list box. Choose **OK**.

WordPerfect will tell you when to insert the disks. Give it whichever disk it asks for. This will go on for a while. (Here's a golden opportunity to fill out your registration card.) When it's all finished, a dialog box will appear asking if you want to read the ReadMe files or not. Choose No if you're like me and you never read the ReadMe files. You just want to get on with the program. You can look at the ReadMe files later if you want.

Choose Exit, then **OK**. Now WordPerfect 6.0 for Windows is installed on your system and you can start reading Lesson 1.

Index

D

K

L

M

N-O

P

Q-R

S

T

U-V

W-Z